Why Do Bluebirds Hate Me?

WHY DO BLUEBIRDS

HATE ME?

More Answers to Common and Not-So-Common
Questions about Birds and Birding

Mike O'Connor

Edited by **Olivia H. Miller**
Illustrations by **Michael Chesworth**

Beacon Press, Boston

Beacon Press
25 Beacon Street
Boston, Massachusetts 02108-2892
www.beacon.org

Beacon Press books
are published under the auspices of
the Unitarian Universalist Association of Congregations.

16 15 14 13   8 7 6 5 4 3 2 1

This book is printed on acid-free paper that meets the uncoated paper
ANSI/NISO specifications for permanence as revised in 1992.

Library of Congress Cataloging-in-Publication Data

O'Connor, Mike, 1953-
  Why do bluebirds hate me? : more answers to common and not-so-
common questions about birds and birding / by Mike O'Connor ; edited
by Olivia H. Miller.
     pages cm
  ISBN 978-0-8070-1253-6 (alk. paper)—ISBN 978-0-8070-1254-3 (ebook)
  1. Bird watching—Miscellanea. 2. Birds—Miscellanea. I. Miller, Olivia
H., editor. II. Title.
  QL677.5.O29 2013
  598.072'34—dc23
                              2013004631

CONTENTS

3.
A Few Things Even You Can Do

4.
There's More to Life Than the Backyard

5.

Bet You Didn't Know Birds Did This

6.

Don't Forget Cities Have Birds, Too

7.

Being Free as a Bird Isn't Always That Great

8.

Birds Are Superstars—and Publishers and Hollywood Know It

9.

A Bird Buffet

INTRODUCTION

Exactly the Same, Only Different

When I mentioned to a friend that I was putting together another book, he asked what this new book would be about. His response caught me off guard. We have been friends for a long time. He knows me pretty well and is aware that I don't know much else once the topic gets beyond birds. Still, I understand why he was asking. After all, I had already written one bird Q&A book. Does the world really need a sequel?

My response to that is, yes, of course it does. (How else do you think I was going to answer that?) I don't know when the first cookbook came out, but cookbooks didn't end with that original book. They still keep coming. There will always be newer and yummier recipes to write about. This same principle applies to bird Q&A books. I've been operating a birding store for over thirty years, and hardly a day goes by when I don't hear a question I've never heard before. Some questions are trivial, some are intriguing, and a few truly scare me.

One of the main reasons for this sequel is that sometimes people want to ask a question but it takes them a while to work up the nerve. It's like when we go to the local auditorium to hear someone speak about some topic (birds, flowers, pet hypnotism) that we thought we were interested in at the time. Sometimes the talks are enlightening, and sometimes they make us wish we had stayed home and done the laundry.

But whether the talks are good or bad, they all end the same way: the speaker's last four words are always, "Anyone have a question?" For the next eight seconds the room is filled with deadly silence. Half the people in the audience want to ask a question but are too self-conscious to be the first to raise a hand; the other half of the audience are praying that no one raises a hand so they can get the heck out of there, or at least be first to the refreshment table.

This book was written for the first half of the audience. It is for the people who were too shy to raise a hand and thus their question didn't make it into my previous book, *Why Don't Woodpeckers Get Headaches? And Other Bird Questions You Know You Want to Ask.* I realize this book should have come out sooner, but I've been busy hanging out at the refreshment table with the other half of the audience. They're my kind of people.

Writing a Q&A bird column for Cape Cod's weekly newspapers is not as easy as it sounds. There are always issues to deal with. For example, some folks insist I get right to the point and give them a straight answer. Others don't like seeing their name in print. First of all, I never give a straight answer, so making such stipulations is a waste of time. Second, relax. I use only first names. No matter how lame the question is, no one is going to know you asked it. I'm sure there is more than one Mary or Rick in, say, Tallahassee. Besides, having your name appear in a bird column is not the worst thing in the world. It's not like having your name in the police blotter or the obituaries. Asking questions about birds is nothing to be ashamed of. It's not as bad as admitting to being from Tallahassee.

One of my favorite ways to receive a question is what I call the "clandestine approach." Someone will catch my eye at work and motion for me to come over to a dark corner of the store. They want to talk to me privately. Suddenly, I feel like I'm about to receive national secrets from Deep Throat. But instead of secrets, I'm asked which is the last bird to go to bed at night or why wrens have such weird tails. Edgy stuff. Soon I understand why these people don't want to be overheard by anyone else.

In this book I've tried to answer the questions that didn't make it in the first time around. I've also included questions from the shy, the paranoid, and the clandestine types. I address such burning topics as these: Why do hummingbirds hum? Why do doves' wings whistle? Do woodpeckers take baths? (Again with the woodpeckers.) I also add a few columns on birds that many folks aren't familiar with. (Ever see a Hoopoe?) It's my way of trying to expand the readers' bird horizons. There's life beyond backyard chickadees and wren tails, you know.

I'm often asked what is the strangest question I've ever gotten, to which I reply, "That question." (It always leads to puzzled looks.) However, I think the top contender for the strangest question has to be one I found on my answering machine one morning. (I swear this is true.) A lady called wanting to know if thistle (nyjer) seed is safe for humans to eat. It seems this woman had bought a bag of thistle, took it home, and put it in a different container to keep it fresh. The next morning she found her houseguest chowing down a bowl of fresh thistle. We played her call over and over until the tape wore out. (I'm starting to understand why some people have second thoughts about asking me questions.) The person who ate the seed suffered no ill effects, BTW, but reportedly now sleeps by standing on one leg and sings very early in the morning.

One last thing: When my first book was released, some folks complained that the illustrations didn't match the text. They suggested that when I wrote about a Belted Kingfisher, for example, it would have been helpful if an appropriate illustration had accompanied the text. In this new book I responded to those complaints by ignoring them. There are tons of precisely illustrated books out there. I didn't want to compete with them. It just wouldn't be fair to those other books. Besides, illustrations cost money. If the publisher put extra dough into illustrations, there wouldn't be enough left to pay me. I certainly can't have that.

1.

Birds Everyone Should Know

Like many books, this first chapter starts off simple and basic. I've avoided dealing with questions about obscure birds or technical topics. Instead, I open with info on comfort birds such as hummingbirds, catbirds, and wrens. There's no point in scaring people on page one.

Why Do Bluebirds Hate Me?

Dear Bird Folks,

I'm a good person. I make my bed every day, floss regularly, and never litter, but bluebirds avoid me and I don't know why. I have a wonderful tree-filled yard with several specially designed bluebird houses, yet I've never seen a single one of those sweet birds anywhere near my yard. On the other hand, my cousin, who lives in the very next town, has lots of them. Why do bluebirds hate me?

—*Roger,* GROTON, CT

It's a tough one, Roger,

It's hard to know why birds don't like certain people, but I'm sure they have their reasons. Do you have a feather pillow or wear a down jacket? Using those things can go against you. What about your favorite superhero? It's not Catwoman, is it? You and I may think she's hot, but birds can't get past her name. Maybe your birdhouses are the problem. Did you buy them from a birding specialty shop or at a creepy hardware store? Birds really hate people who don't buy their houses from specialty shops. And when I say "birds," I mean me. (Sometimes I project.)

I'm going to answer your no-bluebird question by telling you a little story. Years ago I tried to get into fishing. This was back before I decided fish looked more majestic swimming free than gasping for air at the bottom of a bucket. When it comes to a new hobby, I'm one of those guys who spends more time shopping for equipment than actually participating in the hobby itself. I bought a fancy new fishing rod and reel, lots of lures, and even a pair of those jumbo rubber wading boots that make everyone look like Humpty Dumpty. Each morning I would head off to a nearby pond, carrying my new rod and sporting my Humpty Dumpty outfit . . . but I never caught a single fish.

After weeks of frustration, someone told me what my problem was. The pond I kept returning to didn't have any fish in it. Apparently, not all ponds have fish. Who knew? By then it was too late. I had become discouraged, gave up fishing, and moved on to an even crazier hobby—bird watching.

As with fish, birds are habitat specific. For example, Hermit Thrushes like forested areas, sandpipers like mudflats, and meadowlarks like open fields. Eastern Bluebirds fit into the latter category. Farmland, orchards, golf courses, and power line right-of-ways are the bluebirds' habitats of choice, especially during the breeding season. Why do they like open areas so much? It has to do with their feeding preferences. Bluebirds love insects, but instead of picking bugs out of the air like swallows and flycatchers do, they take a less energetic approach.

Bluebirds hunt much the same way Red-tailed Hawks hunt mice and rabbits. They sit on branches that overlook open areas and carefully scan for prey. But instead of looking for rabbits and mice, bluebirds watch for crickets, grasshoppers, or some other buggy things. Once prey is spotted, the bluebird will swoop to the ground and crunch down on a fresh cricket. Bluebirds might seem like "sweet" birds, Roger, but crickets have a different take on them.

Living far from the bluebirds' habitat of choice makes it tough to entice them to use the birdhouses in your yard. It's not your fault and don't blame your birdhouses. If you don't live in the right location, you could put out birdhouses designed by Frank Lloyd Wright and bluebirds still wouldn't use them. (Actually, a birdhouse designed by F. L. Wright would probably frighten the birds, but you get my point.)

Before you become depressed and decide to jump off the roof of one of your trophy birdhouses, I have some good news. Just because your yard isn't prime bluebird-nesting habitat doesn't mean these birds won't pay you a visit other times of the year. During the colder months, bluebirds switch from insects to a healthier fruit diet. When it snows they forget about the crickets and start looking for berries on plants such as American Holly, winterberry, sumac, and hackberry. (Hackberry? Isn't that a respiratory illness kids get?)

In winter, bluebirds form flocks that travel about looking for food. Often these flocks visit areas that aren't typical bluebird habitat. We get far more calls from people reporting bluebirds in their yards in the winter than in the summer. In addition to berries, customers report bluebirds coming for hulled sunflower seed and suet. The birds are also drawn to heated birdbaths.

Actually, fresh water is one of the best ways to attract bluebirds in any season, but I don't like telling people that. There's no money to be made selling birdbath water to the public. People have gotten so cheap lately.

Bluebirds don't hate you, Roger, but they may not love where you live. Instead of investing in more fancy birdhouses, my advice is to plant some holly, sumac, winterberry, or hackberry . . . just keep it away from the kids. In addition, put out hulled sunflower and suet, and keep your birdbath ice-free all winter. You may not get bluebirds to nest in your boxes, but perhaps you could attract them to visit you in the off-season. The sight of a dozen bluebirds eating on a snow-covered holly tree or splashing in your birdbath will quickly make you forget all about your unused nest boxes. If it makes you feel any better, I don't get bluebirds in my yard either. But let's keep that just between you and me. I have an image to protect. I'm still trying to live down the image of me wearing Humpty Dumpty fishing boots.

Woodpeckers Do Take Baths

Dear Bird Folks,
Several species of woodpeckers regularly come to the feeders in our yard. We have Downy and Hairy Woodpeckers, plus red-bellies and flickers. However, I've never seen them use our birdbath. Other birds bathe frequently, but not woodpeckers. Do they take baths?
—Jennifer, EASTHAM, MA

Perfect, Jennifer,

A few years ago I wrote a book entitled *Why Don't Woodpeckers Get Headaches?* It was a huge hit and became the best-selling book (with that exact title) of all time. Since then, I've been thinking about writing a sequel but couldn't come up with a good name . . . until now. *Why Don't Woodpeckers Take Baths?* is perfect. It could lead to a whole series: *Why Don't Woodpeckers Watch TV?* followed by *Why Don't Woodpeckers Use Public Transportation?* and *Why Don't Woodpeckers Shop at the Gap?* Not only are these great titles, but people everywhere will want to know the answers. Forget those silly vampire books; thanks to you, woodpecker mania is about to sweep the country.

When it comes to bathing, not all birds are the same. Like people, some birds constantly wash themselves, while others don't do it nearly as much as we wish they would. Take robins, for example. They seem to be the clean freaks of the bird world; there isn't a birdbath they won't stop at. Starlings must have some Japanese in them because the entire flock often bathes together. But unlike the Japanese version, a starling communal bath isn't a peaceful, relaxing affair. When a flock of starlings hits a birdbath, it's like starting a blender without the cover.

Birds of prey are more humanlike in their bathing habits. Hawks often walk into a pool of water and soak for a bit before getting on with the actual washing. The more sophisticated hawks light candles, put on soft music, and pour a glass of wine before they bathe, but those birds are mostly from Europe. Swallows and swifts do the opposite. With no time in their busy schedules to be floating around, they bathe on the wing. Swallows skim over a pond, flying just low enough to allow the water to splash on them as they go.

Other birds seem to have a touch of hydrophobia; they want to bathe but hate getting into water, so they take a "leaf bath" instead. No, they don't roll around in a big pile of leaves (that behavior is exclusive to ten-year-old children). After a storm, or when there is a lot of morning dew, many warblers bathe by fluttering in wet foliage. Other birds are content to let the bath come to them.

If it rains, they'll readily take advantage of the falling water to clean up. If it doesn't rain, they stay dirty . . . just like ten year olds.

Woodpeckers probably use a combination of those methods to maintain their feathers. Punch up YouTube on the computer and you should find several video clips of downies, flickers, and other woodpeckers splashing in birdbaths. (There's also a fun clip of Woody Woodpecker trying to fish a dime out of a bathtub drain. It has nothing to do with your question, but watch it anyway.) Woodpeckers not only use birdbaths, but they also take the aforementioned rain baths. In the winter they take snow baths, which are exactly as the name implies.

Woodpeckers have also been known to take dust baths. It seems like a major contradiction for birds to clean themselves by rolling in dirt, but they do. Experts aren't sure what the birds gain from fluffing in filth, but they surmise it has something to do with parasite control. It is thought the fine dust blocks the parasites' breathing holes, which forces them to drop off the bird. I'm going to have to try that myself. I'll let you know if it works.

No matter what type of bath woodpeckers take, their next move is always the same: they find a quiet spot where they can do some serious preening to remove any mites or parasites. They also repair damaged feathers by "zipping" them up. (Birds' feathers are like organic Velcro with barbs and hooks that hold each feather together. Sometimes the barbs and hooks separate and need to be "rezipped," which the birds do with their beaks. It's lucky they have those beaks. What bird can afford a tailor these days?) The most important thing they do when preening is oil their feathers. The birds squeeze a bit of oil from an oil gland that is located at the base of their tails and apply it to their feathers. It is commonly thought that the oil provides waterproofing, but it's actually a conditioner that prevents the feathers from becoming dry and brittle . . . and from getting those dreaded split ends.

After further review, Jennifer, I don't think I can call my next book *Why Don't Woodpeckers Take Baths?* They probably bathe more than you realize. I'll have to come up with a new title. In the meantime, I'm going to watch that Woody Woodpecker clip. I can't wait to see if he finally gets the dime out of the tub drain.

Hip Catbirds

Dear Birds Folks,
One of my favorite birds is the Gray Catbird. Its sweet personality really brightens my day. My book says catbirds are "mimics," just like mockingbirds, but I don't agree. I can easily hear other birds' songs coming from mockingbirds, but all I hear from catbirds is an assortment of twitters and tweets. Why are they called mimics?
—*Shawn,* AUBURN, MA

You're kidding me, Shawn,

You don't hear catbirds doing any mimicking? Really? I think they are the best impressionists ever. They are excellent copycats. That last line should give you a hint. Do you get it? "Copy-*cats*"? Meow? Catbirds don't have the word "cat" in their name because they like to scratch expensive furniture, eat stinky canned food, or cough up fur balls. They are called catbirds because they do a great impression of a cat. I know catbirds don't really try to impersonate cats. It's merely a coincidence that the two creatures sound alike. And even though most readers already knew this fact, I felt I had to set the record straight in case anyone reading this is a purist . . . or a purrist.

You're right about mockingbirds. When it comes to imitating other birds' songs, the Northern Mockingbird is the champ. When a mockingbird sings like a robin or a cardinal, it sounds like a

robin or a cardinal. Their replications are so good they have been known to fool professional birders (okay, maybe just me). Catbirds, on the other hand, find this precise singing boring. There is no soul or interpretation. When a catbird sings, it combines the songs of several different birds and then adds a few notes of its own. The end result is a long combination of improvised notes, creating a song that is unique and unlikely to be repeated. Catbirds have the creativity of jazz singers. (I'm talking about good jazz singers, not the kind who give everyone headaches.)

Catbirds are also crepuscular. I know that sounds like a skin infection, but it means they are active before sunrise and after sunset. They are one of the first birds to sing in the morning and one of the last to finally shut up and go to bed. Their songs also tend to be long. A single song may last ten minutes or more, with the occasional guitar solo in the middle. Each song may contain bits from dozens of other birds.

However, the exact number of songs copied is difficult to know, since catbirds often add their own interpretation to each note. In most cases, the notes they sing are taken from local birds, but occasionally they'll incorporate songs from birds that live thousands of miles away. When catbirds return from Central America in the spring, some of them can be heard singing the songs of birds found only in the tropics. I wonder if this bugs the local birds. You know, like when an American returns from England, suddenly speaking with a British accent. What's up with that, guv'nor?

Mockingbirds typically sing from exposed perches, making sure every bird knows about their territory. Catbirds aren't as showy. They often sing while hidden in dense foliage. But that doesn't mean they are shy. In fact, they are one of the few birds that actually seem to like humans. This morning, when I was filling feeders at the store, a catbird flew down and landed at my feet (really). It stared up at me as I filled the feeders (yes, really). Suddenly, it noticed I had left the back door open, took a few hops, and went inside (again, really). Being a stupid human, I did what all stupid humans do and tried talking to it. "Come on out, Mr. Catbird," I begged, but the catbird pretended not to understand. After a few minutes of looking around, the bird flew out of the store without buying anything. (Although it must plan to return because it left a few "deposits" on some expensive items.)

Catbirds do mimic the songs of other birds, Shawn. However, it's fair to say that their version of a particular bird's song isn't as identifiable as a song sung by the mimic master, the mockingbird. A catbird's song is more impressionistic because it likes to include an additional assortment of twitters and tweets. (I'm talking about avian twitters and tweets, not those annoying "twitters" and "tweets" we have to hear about from celebrities.)

What's with All the Grackles?

Dear Bird Folks,
A few days ago we had hundreds (no kidding) of grackles in our
yard. It was scary, like a scene from Albert Hitchcock's movie The
Birds. *What gives?*

—*Ed and Marguerite,* BREWSTER, MA

Yo, Ed and Marguerite,

I hate to be fussy, but the guy who made that blasphemous movie was *Alfred* Hitchcock, not Albert. Albert was Alfred's younger brother. Albert didn't make movies. He worked all his life to become a prince, but unfortunately, things didn't work out. Within a week of reaching his goal, Prince Albert tragically ended up in a can. To this day, no one has let Prince Albert out of the can, no matter how many thirteen-year-old boys call and ask. If you don't know what I'm talking about, ask the nearest thirteen-year-old boy. They have been making that same prank phone call, with that same punch line, since the telephone was invented. If you don't believe me, Marguerite, ask Ed. I bet he made that same prank call when he was a kid, if they had telephones back then.

The grackles were migrating, or at least getting ready to migrate. Late October is their time to head south. And judging from the complaints I get about them, this year's grackle migration couldn't have come soon enough. We get more complaints about grackles than any other creature, except, of course, squirrels. (Squirrels are still, and will always be, the gold standard by which all backyard creature complaints are measured.) Grackles are so unloved that the only creatures that hang with them are other grackles. Usually if you see one grackle, you'll see a bunch. During the summer they travel in family groups but during migration they can be found in flocks of hundreds.

The Common Grackle is one of the most abundant birds in North America, but that wasn't always the case. Grackles don't do well in dense forests, so there weren't nearly as many before the European settlers arrived. That changed once clear-cutting began. The explosion of farms and farmlands caused an explosion in the grackle population. Today there are millions of grackles throughout the eastern half of North America, and they all love our bird feeders. But our grackle issues are nothing compared with what farmers deal with. It seems grackles have the habit of pulling seeds out of the ground just after the farmer plants them. For some reason, farmers don't like that.

Grackles also have a few other nasty habits up their sleeves. They have been known to follow robins and steal worms right out of their beaks, or grab the occasional egg or nestling out of a nest. They may even occasionally kill adult birds, especially House Sparrows. Before you totally hate grackles, you should know that like most things in life, grackles have a good side. They consume huge amounts of annoying pests, including Japanese beetles, grasshoppers, caterpillars, and, of course, House Sparrows.

One of the grackles' less gruesome feeding habits is eating acorns. Some acorn-eating birds, like ducks, simply swallow acorns whole and let their gizzards do the work. Other birds, like jays, open acorns by smashing them apart with their beaks. Grackles have their own unique way of opening acorns. Inside their beaks is a sharp ridge called a "keel," which opens acorns like a can opener opens cans. (Maybe grackles can use their keel to get Prince Albert out of his can.)

Enjoy the migrating grackles, Ed and Marguerite. It's the last you'll see of them until next March, when they return from the south, ushering in the spring and triggering a whole new load of customer complaints. While they are gone, the squirrels will have work to twice as hard to fill the annoyance void. Don't worry, though. It's a challenge they are more than capable of meeting.

Why Hummingbirds Hum

Dear Bird Folks,
Without getting into the old joke, I'd like to know if hummingbirds
sing. I've heard their wings buzz when I'm outside filling their
feeder, but I've never heard them sing, or say anything for that
matter. Do they even talk?

—*Dale,* SCRANTON, PA

Hey, Dale,

I have a question for you: Do you know why hummingbirds hum? Because they don't know the words. There, I did it. I know you said you didn't want to get "into the old joke," but I told it anyway. You're not the boss of me. If there's a joke—new, old, good, bad or terrible—I'm going for it. Besides, there are so few bird jokes, I can't possibly pass up an opportunity. It's not like I'm writing about lawyers, priests, or rabbis. Birds aren't that funny. In fact, they rarely, if ever, walk into a bar.

I think most folks will agree that hummingbirds are amazing. But for all their amazingness, there are a few things they don't do well. They can barely walk, their swimming skills are limited, and they are lousy singers. When was the last time you heard someone complain about being woken up early by singing hummingbirds? It's not that they don't try to sing. Every morning, a male Ruby-throated Hummingbird flies to an exposed branch in his breeding territory and sings his heart out. But instead of sounding like a nightingale, he sounds more like Andy Devine. A couple of raspy growls and chirps are all he can muster. Even I sing better than that.

Female hummingbirds have their own territory to defend, but they handle things differently. When a mother hummer is sitting on her nest and notices an intruder, she typically remains quiet. Her hope is that the other hummingbird will pass by without

incident. However, if the encroaching bird decides to hang out for a while and sip from the local flowers, she'll be forced to do something. She's not about to share her limited food supply with some lowlife moocher. When the female decides enough is enough, she springs into action. There are no caution chirps uttered or warning shots fired. Instead, the female launches herself at the interloper like a winged dart. In most cases, the startled invader quickly flies away—far away—to someplace where it can catch its breath and try to figure out what just happened.

When mom is away, the nestlings remain quiet and sit motionless. Upon returning, she will signal that everything is safe by giving a few soft chirps. The instant they hear her voice, they pop up, open their mouths, and whine, "What took you so long? We're hungry!" (Adult hummingbirds are only able to chirp softly, but their kids speak perfect English. Amazing.)

Young hummingbirds are the yappiest of them all. As they leave the nest and take their first flight, they can't contain themselves. They shriek and scream like human kids on the last day of school. In their excitement to see the world, they often ignore the warning calls of the adults in neighboring territories. Adult hummingbirds don't have a soft spot in their hearts for other birds' kids. If a young bird stumbles into the wrong territory, it is quickly attacked by the current landlord. Fortunately, young hummers are fast learners. After getting whacked upside the head a few times, they learn which areas to avoid.

Even though hummingbirds have poor singing skills, they are experts in nonverbal communication. Like most birds, hummers are able to puff out and spread their tail feathers to appear bigger and badder. They can also increase the intensity of the humming made by their wings to further announce their displeasure.

Male hummingbirds have their own special trick. They flash their gorget. I know flashing a gorget sounds like something Brett Favre got in trouble for doing, but it's different with hummingbirds. The gorget is a colorful patch most male hummers have in their throats. When sunlight strikes the male Ruby-throated Hummingbird's gorget at just the right angle, it changes from an uninteresting dark spot to a brilliant red beacon. The red gorget acts like an avian stop sign, telling other hummers to halt and go back to wherever they came from. Most birds heed this warning; but if they don't, they get whacked upside the head.

Hummingbirds do talk, Dale. While their vocal range is limited to squeaks and chirps, they are able to get their point across by adding flashing colors and sounds produced by their wings, and using the tail-feather trick to double their size. Now that I've answered your question, I'll get ready to answer next week's question, which I'm sure will be either "What is the correct formula for hummingbird food" (four parts water to one part sugar) or "Who the heck is Andy Devine?"

Carolina Wrens Singin' in the Fall

Dear Bird Folks,
I read in your column that birds sing in the spring to attract a mate. The Carolina Wrens in my yard apparently don't read your column because they are singing more than ever. Why are these birds singing now (in the fall)? Are they late nesters or just mixed up?
—Ralph, ANNAPOLIS, MD

Good for you, Ralph,

While I'm not happy to learn that wrens aren't reading my column, I have to give you credit. You correctly observed that many birds have quieted down. In the fall the only birds we usually hear are crows and a few jays. Suddenly, however, the little Carolina Wrens have become nearly as loud as the crows, and that's loud. One wren in my yard was so noisy I could hear it singing while I blasted my stereo. It's hard to distract me when I'm rocking out to the Partridge Family, but this bird can do it.

What I wrote about birds singing is true. They sing in the spring to attract a mate, but they also sing to announce their territories. Most birds vigorously defend a breeding territory but back off as soon as the nesting season is over. Birds are like pro athletes. When it's game time, they hate each other, but as soon as the action stops, all the blustering comes to an end. Then they hang out and compare commercial endorsements. The feisty Carolina Wrens aren't that phony; they hate each other year-round, 24/7/365, and then some.

Carolina Wrens are the only wrens in the East that don't migrate. The idea of making those long, dangerous flights, packing and unpacking, stopping the mail delivery, and draining the water pipes for the winter is too much. When they find a location they like, they stay there and never leave. The only thing they have to do is defend their location from other Carolina Wrens.

Right now you might be thinking: "If these wrens don't migrate, where would the other wrens come from? Shouldn't everybody have a place to live?" Throughout most of the year that may be true, but in the fall thousands of newly hatched wrens are looking for a home. Good luck to them. Finding a new territory won't be easy. The best places are already taken, and they'll be chased away if they get too close to another bird's claim. Young Carolina Wrens are the skateboarders of the bird world. They aren't doing anything wrong, yet they are constantly told to move on.

While most songbirds form couples in the spring, Carolina Wrens often pair up in the fall. Finding and holding a productive territory is critical to their survival during the coming winter. They need to pair up because a new wren couple has a much better chance of defending a territory than a single male does, and a single female has no chance at all. (Sorry, libbers, that's just the way it is.)

Naturally landscaped yards with lots of thickets, leaf litter, and a brush pile or two are appealing to Carolina Wrens. You are less likely to find them in manicured yards, like the ones featured on the cover of *Pesticide Monthly*. They'll also use birdhouses, but they are more likely to build a nest where you'd least expect it, and often where you'd rather they didn't. Planters, mailboxes, and flowerpots have been used; covers of propane tanks are one of their favorite, and most annoying, places. This year I've had two customers come in with coffee cans that had been used by nesting wrens. Wrens in coffee cans? That explains their hyperness.

Enjoy your wrens, Ralph. It's nice to hear a few birds singing late into the fall. And by the way, it's only the males you hear singing. Again, sorry, ladies, but that's just the way it is.

Titmice Love Peanuts but Hate Water

Dear Bird Folks,
I have several Tufted Titmice coming to my yard. I give them whole peanuts still in the shell. The birds take the peanuts and fly away. My question is: Do they eat the peanuts or do they hide them someplace for later? I'm wondering because they sure take a lot of peanuts for such small birds.

—*Peg*, BREWSTER, MA

You have lucky birds, Peg,

They get peanuts. The birds in my yard get nothing but the same monotonous sunflower seeds, day in and day out. In this economy, that's all I can afford—and sometimes they don't even get that. Occasionally, I have to leave an IOU. The birds aren't happy but they understand. They know things are tough. There was a time when I could afford to put out peanuts, too. It was back in the roaring nineties, and Bernie Madoff hadn't stolen everybody's money yet.

I'm glad you asked about titmice. They are totally underrated birds. While cardinals, hummingbirds, and bluebirds grab all the headlines, the lowly titmouse regularly comes and brightens up our yards with little fanfare. It's probably their generic gray plumage and bland personalities that cause us to take them for granted. The only thing that makes these birds stand out is their wacky name. (Whose idea was that?) But beneath all their plainness Tufted Titmice are tough and interesting birds.

Let's begin by talking about their toughness. Titmice are nonmigratory. That means the birds you see at your feeder in July are most likely the same birds you'll see clinging to your feeder during a February nor'easter. Right now you may be wondering, "What's so special about that? Chickadees are smaller than titmice and they are out in the same nasty weather." That's true, but chickadees have been around here for centuries and have had time to evolve ways to deal with our nasty weather. Titmice are basically southern birds and are fairly new to New England. The first titmice didn't breed in Massachusetts until 1958, when a pair nested in a place called "Waban." I don't know how they found Waban, because I've lived in Massachusetts all my life and I've never heard of it. Waban? Who named it? Elmer Fudd?

In order to survive New England's—and Waban's—frigid winters, titmice gather food in the fall and stash it away for the winter; that's exactly what they were doing with your pricey peanuts. Each nut is removed from its shell and then carefully hidden in a crevice or under a piece of tree bark. With any luck, the food the birds worked so hard to store this fall will be waiting for them when winter's snow and ice cover their natural food supply.

Tufted Titmice may be unafraid to face winter head-on, but there is one thing they are afraid of, and it's rather surprising. Titmice hate water . . . at least they hate to fly over it. Even a body of water as narrow as the Cape Cod Canal is too scary for titmice to cross. So how did these birds ever colonize the Cape without flying over the canal? They got here the same way we do; they used the bridges. In the seventies, when the titmice on the mainland had a population explosion, witnesses claimed to have seen dozens of titmice moving across the bridges. The birds flew from one girder to the next, slowly working their way across the bridges until they reached the other side. Apparently, the birds were willing to do anything to get out of Waban.

Once on the Cape, the birds settled in and their population grew rapidly. However, the nearby island of Nantucket still has no Tufted Titmice; these hydrophobic birds won't fly across Nantucket Sound. Tiny hummingbirds annually make the five-hundred-mile trip across the Gulf of Mexico, while the much larger titmice refuse to make the short fifteen-mile flight to Nantucket. At least, I think it's the water that's keeping them away. Maybe the birds just don't want to go to Nantucket. They heard what those people did to the whales.

I'm glad you're enjoying the titmice, Peg. It's nice to know someone appreciates them. After all, there's nothing wrong being gray and a little bland. Look how far it's gotten me.

No-Bird Syndrome

Dear Bird Folks,

For the past few months, I have been getting tons of birds at my feeders. Suddenly, they stopped coming. I haven't changed anything. I'm still using the same feeders and the same special seed mixture, which I buy locally. What is going on? Has anything happened to the birds?

—Kristen, READING, MA

You're lucky, Kris,

Fortunately for you, I'm too busy wondering if they pronounce the name of your town "Redding" or "Reeding" to give you a hard time for using "special seed mixture." You know how I hate that stuff. To make things worse, you buy your mixed seed from some other store. If you are going to buy crappy seed, you could at least buy it from me. My mixed seed is just as lousy as the next guy's. And while I'd love to blame your lack of birds on your birdseed, this is simply not the case. Blame the calendar; June is not a feeder-friendly month.

There are two months each year when "no-bird syndrome" strikes the feeder world. The first is December, when many birds have migrated and lots of natural food is still available. December is also the month when many old-schoolers traditionally begin to feed birds for the season. (For some reason, they think birds only eat in certain seasons.) Combine fewer birds, lots of natural food, and more feeder choices, and we have fewer birds at our feeders.

The second "no-bird" month is June. Now everyone is thinking, "June? How can that be? All the birds are back, and the old-schoolers have put their feeders away. Why is June bad?" June is noted for three things: weddings, graduations, and lots and lots of bugs. No matter what kind of superfood we put in our feeders, we can't compete with juicy, squishy bugs.

19

As I write this, the birdhouse outside my window is filled with baby chickadees. About fifty feet from this crowded birdhouse is a bird feeder filled with food. (I'm talking about good food, not a "special mix" bought from some generic store in Reading . . . however it's pronounced.) I haven't seen a single cardinal, titmouse, nuthatch, or Blue Jay at this feeder. Nor have I seen a single chickadee. You'd think that chickadee parents, with a nest of hungry baby birds, would be visiting a feeder constantly. Nope. Baby birds grow much faster on a diet of protein-packed insects. Seed simply doesn't have the growing power insects do. And like most parents, birds want their kids to grow up and get out of the house as quickly as possible. Thus, bugs, not seeds, are their food of choice.

Right now the most common birds at my feeders are goldfinches, which are vegetarians. They would rather have their kids grow more slowly than allow themselves to partake in the nasty habit of eating meat. I also have a few sparrows, which are mostly vegetarians, and grackles. Grackles are vegetarians, fruitarians, bugtarians, wormarians, breadtarians, and liverwurstarians. June or no June, grackles never pass up free food. That's just how they roll.

I know the lack of feeder birds is disappointing, Kris, but no one feels your pain more than I. June is Death Valley in the bird-food industry. Even in the middle of winter, when the Cape is quiet and most of my customers are sitting in their lanais in Florida, we sell more seed than in June. There's good news, however. Once the baby birds have fledged and are flying around, they'll come to your feeders and they'll be looking for birdseed. In fact, you'll be getting so many birds, you'll think the special mixture you are using is actually good. Trust me, it's not.

Birds Can't Afford Bottled Water

Dear Bird Folks,

I'd like to know where birds get water. There aren't any ponds near my apartment community, but we do have a ceramic water-holder thing on a pedestal. Where do birds find water if humans don't provide any for them or when it doesn't rain for a while?

—*Leslie,* DENNIS, MA

Take it easy, Leslie,

This column is written for novice bird lovers. I like to keep things simple and try to avoid scientific nomenclature. The term "ceramic water holder thing on a pedestal" might be understood by hydrographers and brilliant people like you and me, but for the sake of the other readers, let's just call it a "birdbath." That will keep everyone else from running to the nearest technical journal in an effort to understand what we are talking about.

For years, I've told people they can attract more birds with water than with a bird feeder, and that statement continues to be true. Only a few dozen species are actually interested in our feeders, no matter what birdseed manufacturers tell us. But every bird needs water—to drink and to bathe in. If birds don't keep themselves clean, they run the risk of losing their friends. More importantly, if their feathers aren't kept clean, they will not be able to thermoregulate (i.e., keep themselves warm or cool) and that can be fatal.

When it comes to natural water supplies, there's more fresh water available than most folks realize. If you were to see your town from above, as the birds do, you'd realize that all but arid communities are littered with lakes, small ponds, streams, and other pockets of fresh water. "No Trespassing" signs put up by snobby property owners might work to keep the rest of us out, but they don't bother the birds one bit.

Another thing birds have going for them is morning dew. The same dew we wipe off our lawn furniture each morning is valued by the birds. Hummingbirds especially love to drink droplets of the morning dew that has formed on leaves. Many mornings I've been woken up by the sound of birds landing on my gutters, sipping up pools of moisture formed by the aforementioned dew running off my roof during the night. (Being woken up by the sound of birds in the gutter should not be confused with "waking up in the gutter." That's another story altogether.)

Let's not forget about puddles. They are one of the birds' favorite places to drink and bathe. Even the briefest rain shower will produce a few puddles, and the birds readily take advantage of them. However, puddles have a dangerous downside. Humans seem to be obsessed with toxic chemicals, which can run off into puddles; and the birds pay the price. I'm not talking about industrial runoff. That's another problem. I'm talking about homeowners' runoff. Every time we spray for ants, aphids, moths, and dandelions or wash our cars with some miracle supershine detergent, we are probably using harmful products. And rain carries these toxic products into puddles and is slurped up by trusting cardinals and finches.

Seedeaters typically need to drink more often than carnivores. Predators obtain most of the moisture they require from the juicy meat they consume. That's why we see lots of sparrows but few hawks at our birdbaths (aka, ceramic water-holder thing). But that doesn't mean raptors never drink. One fall I was watching the sunset over a local pond when I spotted a Great Horned Owl on the opposite shore. The owl, too, was enjoying the sunset, but it was also drinking water. It took several long sips from the pond. Seeing an owl drink is rare, and it made me wonder why it was so thirsty, but as the bird flew away I noticed it was carrying a large bag of salted pretzels, which explained everything.

While most locations are fortunate to have an adequate supply of fresh water, Leslie, it doesn't mean we shouldn't put out a birdbath. It's fun to watch birds come to drink and bathe. And if you put out a bag of pretzels, you might even see an owl. Just be careful. Pretzels could also attract that pudgy guy who sits at the end of the bar at the local pub. I don't think you ever want to see him bathing in your ceramic water-holder thing.

Not All Cardinals Are Catholic

Dear Bird Folks,
I hope you don't mind but I have a rather strange question. One of my favorite birds is the cardinal. I would like to know how it got its name. Does it have anything to do with Catholic cardinals or is there a more birdie explanation?

—*Emma*, WHEELING, WV

It's totally fine, Emma,
Don't ever feel bad about asking me a strange question. That's what I live for. Without odd questions, this column would be as interesting as the section of the newspaper that contains the weekly business calendar. (BTW, the Rotary Club breakfast is at 7:00 a.m. . . . again.) But ask a question about birds being Catholic, and you'll have people at the edge of their seats. Just about everyone wants to know the answer to that, especially the birds.

When the early pioneers arrived in North America, they were shocked when they first laid their eyes on cardinals. These birds were way flashier than any of those drab birds the settlers saw in England. And what did they call this new, flashy bird? Unfortunately, the settlers didn't have much in the way of imagination. After the long journey they were too jet lagged and full of scurvy to think of anything clever, so they simply called this new species the "red bird."

While the name lacked originality, it seemed to fit the bird just fine. Well, until they spotted a Scarlet Tanager. Oops! Suddenly "red bird" didn't work as well. Then a guy (probably Jebediah somebody) suggested they switch the name to "cardinal" because of the similar bright red outfits worn by officials in the Catholic Church. Everybody loved that name. Not only did it describe the bird's color, and thus avoid the pending lawsuit with the tanager, but it also further elevated the bird's stature. It was a win-win. Well, it was for a while.

The name "cardinal" remained unchallenged for hundreds of years. In fact, if you are a "mature" adult like me and still have all your old bird books, you'll notice the books simply call the cardinal, "cardinal." Then in 1983, another guy (probably Jebediah somebody, Jr.) pointed out that South America also has several species of birds with the common name of "cardinal." Nuts! We had to change our cardinal's name again. Several new names were suggested, including "Joe, the Cardinal," "Mr. C," and "Good ole' Rusty," but the name they settled on was "Northern Cardinal." Of course, this new name didn't sit well with everyone. Many southern states, where cardinals are extremely popular, weren't thrilled about calling their favorite bird "northern," but they ultimately decided it was better than calling it Good ole' Rusty.

Now that we've explained where the cardinal got its name, it's time to talk about where the Catholic cardinals' name came from. Catholic cardinal comes from the Latin *cardo,* meaning "hinge." There was a time when these Church officials had great power and many of society's norms and laws "hinged" on their decisions.

The reason why they dress in red isn't as clear. Some say it has to do with power. In the old days, red fabric was rare and expensive. Anyone who could afford red was automatically considered a big shot. Others say cardinals wear red to remind everyone that they would do anything for the Church, including shedding their own blood. Whoa! Still others argue that red is worn strictly for practical reasons: since many of the cardinals reside in Italy, the red outfits were chosen to hide possible stains from spaghetti sauce and thus cut back on laundry bills. I'm sure that's the real reason.

Until bluebirds and hummingbirds usurped them, Northern Cardinals were the backyard bird watcher's favorite birds. The cardinal is so popular that seven U.S. states named it as their state bird. And it was nearly honored by an eighth state when Delaware considered making the cardinal its state bird. But for some reason they changed their minds and chose the "blue hen" instead. That's right. Delaware's state bird is the blue hen. How did that happen? Clearly, some chicken lover paid off a state official (probably Jebediah Perdue).

Anyone who wants to entice cardinals to their yard should know that this bird's favorite food is sunflower seed. They'll eat any type of sunflower, but they seem to really like black oil sunflower. That's good news for consumers, because black oil sunflower is often less expensive than other sunflowers. (So far ExxonMobil hasn't gotten its hands on this kind of black oil.) Another popular food for cardinals is safflower seed. Safflower is a hard white seed, and many other birds don't like dealing with its tough shell, but the cardinal's huge beak can open it effortlessly.

Safflower also has an additional benefit. Many other birds, such as jays and grackles—and even squirrels—aren't particularly fond of safflower and often leave it alone. The key word here is "often," not "always." If you try safflower seed and grackles or squirrels decide to eat it, I don't want to hear from your lawyer.

Now that I've answered your question, Emma, do me a favor: don't tell my mother I said Catholic cardinals wear red to hide spaghetti sauce stains. She'll make me go to confession every day for the rest of the year.

2.

It's Time to Look Past the Feathers

Everybody knows a little something about birds, especially common birds such as swans, doves, and chickens. But even these familiar birds have a hidden side. Once we look past the feathers, it turns out birds have quite interesting lives. Well, interesting if you like such things.

Don't Call Me "Pretty Boy"

Dear Bird Folks,
When I was a kid, I enjoyed visiting my spinster aunt in Cincinnati because she had a pet parakeet, what some people call a "budgie." I've always assumed these parakeets were descendants of wild birds, but I never knew where they came from. My question is: Where are parakeets from, and are they still found in the wild?
—Maura, DAYTON, OH

Me too, Maura,

My aunt also had a pet parakeet. Was your aunt's bird named "Pretty Boy"? Over the years I think my aunt had five different parakeets, and each one was named Pretty Boy. Strangely enough, the birds never seemed to mind. Now that I think about it, years ago everyone seemed to have a spinster aunt who had a parakeet. Back then, parakeets, mothballs, and plastic on the furniture were required equipment for an aunt. Plastic-covered furniture may look tacky, but it probably wasn't a bad idea with Pretty Boy flying around the house.

You are right to assume that parakeets are descendants of wild birds. Some folks believe Woolworth's created parakeets to be sold along with Baggies of live goldfish and turtles with designs painted on their shells, but parakeets are parrots. Most small parrots with pointed tails are typically called parakeets. In the United States when we talk about parakeets, we are most often referring to a specific species of parrot called a Budgerigar. To the rest of the world, Budgerigars are known as "budgies." In 1840 budgies were imported to England from Australia. (In exchange for the birds, England sent Australia convicts.)

The English immediately fell in love with these friendly, cute, spirited little birds. The Brits rewarded the birds' friendliness by capturing thousands more from the wild and locking them in cages. Fortunately for the wild birds, the budgie-importing craze didn't last long, because it was soon discovered that budgies easily bred in captivity. Captive breeding provided millions of birds for Woolworth's and spinster aunts.

Wild budgies have green bodies, checkered backs, and yellow faces. Evidently that look wasn't good enough for breeders, because they soon went about trying to improve on nature. Over the years many flavors of budgies have been produced, including gray, blue, yellow, violet, and tons of colors in between. Once, even bright-red budgies were imported from breeders in India. The British couldn't figure out how the Indians were able to breed red birds until the red birds began to molt. It turns out the Indian birds weren't naturally red but had simply spent the afternoon at the beauty shop. Yes, it was a dye job. Once the molt began and the birds weren't able to touch up their roots, the jig was up.

Wild Budgerigars are native to the grasslands of Australia, where they fly in large flocks. The name Budgerigar comes from an Aborigine word meaning "good meal." (That can't be a good thing.) When the Aborigines came upon a tree filled with roosting budgies, they would snag a few and roast them in the evening's fire. Yah, I wish I didn't know that either.

Most North American songbirds breed in the spring, but budgies don't follow the seasons. Instead, they breed based on the food supply. Much of Australia's interior is dry; whenever rain arrives it leads to the growth of the wild grasses and other seed-producing plants that budgies love. At the first sign of rain, the birds shift into breeding mode.

Breeding budgies show their affection by preening each other. They also feed each other by first eating some food and then regurgitating it into their mate's mouth. I am so glad humans haven't copied that tradition. My wife eats lima beans, and those things are gross even when they are fresh.

I'm not a fan of keeping birds in cages, Maura, but domestic budgies may be the only companionship some people have. I guess there aren't enough personal ads seeking someone who enjoys quiet dinners, long walks on the beach, mothballs, and plastic on the furniture.

Swans Support Integration

Dear Bird Folks,
We've been watching a family of swans in a local pond. In addition
to the parents, there are seven young ones. Two are white, while the
other five are brown. Why aren't all the babies the same color?
—*Marg and Frank,* BREWSTER, MA

It's Cape Cod, Marg and Frank,

If swans want to have white babies and brown babies, no one here is going to stop them. Cape Cod is one of the most tolerant places on earth. Every lifestyle is welcome. Haven't you ever been to Provincetown? Talk about bending the rules. To some extent, even Yankee fans are tolerated here. Can you imagine?

North America has only two native species of swans, and neither is likely to be seen on Cape Cod. The swan we see on our ponds and bays is the introduced Mute Swan. Depending on whom you talk to, they are either creatures of stately beauty or great annoyance (much like me). The peculiar thing is, the public loves them, while the authorities would like to see them disappear. This is a bit ironic, because it's often the officials who push for protection of certain animals, while the public would rather have them eliminated—this is especially true for creatures like coyotes, Canada Geese, Piping Plovers, and Yankee fans.

Mute Swans typically form into pairs in late winter. Once paired up, the two birds usually remain together for life. Divorce among swans is rare, but when it does occur it is most often the result of a failed nesting season. Bird couples that can't reproduce have little reason to be together. Another possible reason for divorce is when the female complains that the male never talks to her, to which the male responds: "Hello? I'm a 'Mute' Swan. You knew that when you married me."

29

Either bird quickly looks for a new mate if the other one dies. Male Mute Swans are willing to accept a younger or older female, but females generally only pick younger males as a new mate. They don't want another old guy dropping dead on them.

When it comes to nest site selection, it's the male's job to find an acceptable location. He usually picks several spots and may even start nest construction on a few of them. But no matter how hard he works, the female ultimately decides where the couple will live. The female lays six eggs on average and does most of the incubating. Only when she goes to find food will the male sit on the eggs. But since he lacks a brood patch (an area of exposed skin on the belly needed to warm the eggs), his egg sitting is mostly so he can tell his friends that he helps out around the nest. After about five weeks, the young swans hatch out of their shells and are ready to take on the world. Here's where things get interesting.

When the proud parents look at their new cygnets, the first thing they may notice is that not all of the kids look alike. Some babies may be all white, while others may be gray. The shocked adult birds then turn to each other with a suspicious look, to which they simultaneously say, "Don't look at me."

Producing cygnets in assorted colors may at first indicate fowl (get it?) play but it's actually normal. For some reason, Marg and Frank, cygnets have two color morphs. For the first few months of their lives, young swans may be either white or gray/brown. But no matter which color they begin with, eventually all the babies grow to look like their parents—very handsome and totally white, which explains why swans are such bad dancers.

Sandhill Cranes Migrate (Mostly)

Dear Bird Folks,

About a month ago I watched a nature show on migrating Sand-hill Cranes. The program talked about massive flocks pushing north each spring. However, I've just recently returned from a bird-ing trip in Florida, where I was told that Sandhill Cranes don't migrate. What gives?

—James, FALMOUTH, MA

Here's what gives, Jim,

The show you watched is correct. Sandhill Cranes migrate. And what you heard in Florida is also correct. Many of those cranes don't ever leave the state. They don't migrate because Flo-ridian Sandhill Cranes tend to be older and pull up their pants so high above their waists they have trouble flying. In addition, according to a recent study, many of the Florida cranes miss the annual migration because when it's time to go they are in the den napping. It's a chronic problem in that part of the country.

You aren't the only person who saw that show, James. I've had several folks ask me why some cranes migrate, while others are sedentary. I wonder if the cranes realize their migration habits have become such a hot topic. As with most things in the bird world, nothing is simple. Sandhill Cranes consist of six different subspecies, three of which don't ever migrate. The populations of nonmigratory cranes are rather small and are found in Mis-sissippi, Florida, and Cuba (although I doubt the Cuban cranes would be allowed to leave even if they wanted to).

The migratory cranes spend the winter in the southern half of the United States and northern Mexico. Each spring, the migrant birds fly north to their breeding grounds in Michigan, Minnesota, Wisconsin, Alaska, Canada, and eastern Siberia. Along the way, an estimated 500,000 northbound Sandhill Cranes, 80 percent

of their population, stop along a seventy-five-mile stretch of Nebraska's Platte River. It's a spectacular sight, but also very loud. The call of a single crane is an intense bugle-like sound that can be heard for miles. Imagine the sound of 500,000 of them. And my neighbors complain when I play my Monkees albums too loud.

Unlike many migrating birds, Sandhill Crane couples remain together year-round, even in a huge flock. The advantage of staying together is the birds are ready to get down to business the minute they reach their breeding grounds. But before mating, they must perform their wacky "crane dance," which helps solidify their pair bond. During the dance, the pair will rear their heads back and make a series of those raucous calls we talked about earlier. They then bounce, twirl, leap, flap and bow, all in uneven, spastic motions, looking like marionettes controlled by a puppeteer on acid, or me trying to do the Hustle at a wedding.

When the dancing is over, the birds begin building their nest, another goofy process. With their backs to the nest site, they repeatedly toss nesting material over their heads, like someone frantically looking for something in a crowded closet. Once they've accumulated enough material, the female puts an end to all the silliness and starts to form a nest.

Eventually, she lays two eggs, and both adults share in the incubation duties. Just before hatching, the baby birds begin to chirp . . . while still inside the egg. How cute! The cuteness doesn't last long, because Sandhill Crane siblings hate each other from day one. They squabble over everything, especially food and which TV channel to watch. And unless there's an abundance of food, only one chick will survive. On a brighter note, if both chicks can hold on for about a month, they'll slowly learn to live with each other and eventually get along. I'm still waiting for that day with my siblings.

The young cranes remain with their parents for the next year. The adults show them the migration routes, the best places to find food, and how to behave like a proper crane. It takes several years before young cranes are old enough to start their own family, but by the end of the first year their parents have had enough. Before the next breeding season begins, the adults forcefully drive the kids away. It seems cruel, but it's for the best. The young birds shouldn't have to witness all that freaky dancing. No kids want to see their parents doing that.

Bird migration is a complicated thing, James. It would seem to make sense that a species should either be migratory or non-migratory, but different crane populations don't behave the same way when it comes to migration. Nature likes to keep us on our toes.

One last thing about Sandhill Cranes: They may be the oldest bird species alive. An exact fossil, dating back ten million years, has been discovered. I'm not sure where they found this old fossil, but I'm willing to bet it was in Florida, slowly driving down Route 1, looking for the nearest bingo hall.

Quail Chicks Have Two Dads

Dear Bird Folks,
For many years we've had several generations of bobwhites feeding
in our yard. Year after year, mom led her babies through a hole in
our fence to eat. This year has been a little different. We still have a
family of babies coming, but instead of being led by mom, the kids
are led by two dads. Is it unusual for two males to raise a family
of baby birds?

—*CJ, JC,* CHATHAM, MA

You know, CJ, JC,

It's okay to use real names. What's with this "CJ, JC" stuff? It
looks like a text from my kids. I never know what they are saying.
Here's what I get: "Dad, BTW, LOL, $$!, OMG, LBJ, STP, NBC."
Even after staring at it for five minutes, IDK what they are trying
to say. I only understand "Dad" and "$$!," which are all they really want me to understand.

I love that you get an annual family of bobwhites. You are
one of the chosen few. Once upon a time, the calls of bobwhites,
crashing waves, crying gulls, and angry car horns made up the
soundtrack of a Cape Cod summer. But in recent years the car
horns have increased, while sadly, the bobwhites have decreased.
It's nice to know that your yard still gets bobwhites, or as you
probably call them, BWs.

Like many relationships, the mating process of the Northern
Bobwhite is complicated. At first, they seem like the perfect couple. The two birds are inseparable. They sleep, eat, and travel
together, and are always finishing each other's sentences. He says
"bob" and she says "white." (No, not really.) They also participate
in something called "tidbitting." (Yes, you read that right.) Tidbitting is a behavior in which the male picks up a bit of food and of-

fers it to his mate, although some humans interpret this as kissing or a sign of love. Oh, gag.

The quail couple builds their nest on the ground out of soft grasses, and often places dried grass over the top, like a little brown igloo. The whole process only takes a few days, but the birds have to wait for the building inspector, and we all know how long that can take. The female lays about a dozen eggs and purposely won't start incubating the eggs until the last one is laid. Her goal is to have all the eggs hatch simultaneously.

Synchronized hatching is critical, because young bobwhites are nidifugous (and you thought tidbitting was a stupid word). Nidifugous means the babies are up and walking shortly after they hatch. Chicks that hatch late may find the rest of the family has moved on without them, and that's not good. Unless you happen to be that quail, Robert. (Check out "African Eagles Can't Compare to Ours" to see what I mean.)

Most newly hatched songbirds are rather ugly, but baby bobwhites are ridiculously cute from the start. They are about the size of bumblebees (stingerless bumblebees). From day one, they can move about on their own and are able to feed themselves. However, one thing they can't do is regulate their own body temperature. The little quail need to be brooded regularly by their parents, especially at night or during bad weather. Both parents take turns brooding the chicks. Occasionally, one of the adults may decide that this particular family is not for him/her and will abandon one family to start another. As I said, bobwhite relationships are complicated.

It's not uncommon to see a bobwhite family led by both a male and a female, or by a single male or a single female. Single parenting may be the result of divorce, but it could also be due to predation. Just about everything eats quail. Because of the real possibility of losing a parent, baby bobwhites have evolved to survive with only one. But, wait. You said you saw a family led by two males. Only in Massachusetts.

I don't know why your quail family has two dads, CJ, JC, but I have a couple of guesses. The first one is simple. Two different families, led by two different males, have combined to become one big superfamily, like the Brady Bunch. The other suggestion may be the more probable. Throughout the summer, we hear quail saying, "bob-white." These calling birds are usually unattached males hoping against hope to find an available female. Sometimes they get lucky, but often they spend the summer as bachelors.

When they finally give up looking for love, these loser birds turn their attention to finding a flock to hook up with for the winter. Often the flock they find is a family, consisting of several young birds and a parent or two. This may be the case with your birds. The second male is merely a hanger-on and has nothing to do with parenting the babies. I have a feeling, CJ, JC, the extra male you are seeing is one of these bachelor quail. He has no mate, no money, won't leave, and keeps promising he'll get a job but never does. In other words, it's an uncle.

They're Called Snowy Owls for a Reason

Dear Bird Folks,
A few weeks ago you wrote about how tough it is for sea ducks to ride out the winter in the open ocean. I'm wondering if the weather is tougher on inland birds. Ocean water tends to moderate the surrounding air temperature, thus it must be warmer for the ducks than for the birds wintering in the northern forests. Right? Also, which bird species can tolerate the coldest temperature?

—*Rod,* SYRACUSE, NY

Sure, Rod,

If you think inland birds have it tougher than the ducks, so be it. You are from Syracuse, the city that invented winter. When it comes to cold weather, you people know what you are talking about. I recently saw on the news that you had a whopping six feet of snow in the first two weeks of December. Six feet in two weeks! I didn't hear what happened during the second two weeks of the month, but I assume you got even more snow and everyone in the city is dead. After receiving your note, I rethought my assumption. It appears you at least survived. Whew! I hate to lose a reader, even one from Syracuse.

You're right. It is a lot colder inland than near the ocean. Birds that remain in the frozen north have to be extremely hardy. Which bird can tolerate the most cold? I'm not sure, but a prime candidate has to be the Snowy Owl. Snowy Owls have been observed in temperatures that are 80 degrees below zero. That's the air temp, not the wind chill. I set the work thermostat at 62 degrees. I keep it low because I'm environmentally sensitive (plus I'm too cheap pay the heating bill). That temperature seems fine to me, but a few workers and customers complain that they are "freezing." I tell these grumblers that Snowy Owls can survive when the temperature is 142 degrees colder and never complain. So far, this has failed to impress them.

Any birds that can survive eighty degrees below zero would have to be tough and rugged, and Snowy Owls certainly meet these criteria. They are North America's heaviest owls; nearly double the weight of their northern neighbor, the Great Gray Owl. They are also ferocious hunters, eating just about anything that moves, including rabbits, muskrats, Canada Geese, and Great Blue Herons. I once saw a Snowy grab and eat a family from Duluth driving in their Prius, but fortunately those events are rare.

However, the Snowy Owls' number-one food of choice is a delicious lemming. Lemmings are small mammals of the tundra. It has been estimated that a single Snowy Owl may consume sixteen hundred lemmings annually. Even though lemmings are fairly chubby, about the size of a baked potato, the owls can easily swallow one whole. Seeing an owl swallow something that large without chewing would totally freak out my mother. She always nagged us about chewing. Her favorite phrase was we have to "masticate" our food. I never wanted to do that because I was afraid I'd go blind.

Lemming populations are constantly changing. Some years, lemmings are everywhere. During these years the owls are able to breed successfully and raise large families. Other years, there are few lemmings to be found. The powerful birds are somehow able to recognize that food will be in short supply and won't breed at all during the lean years. The owls are smart enough to know they shouldn't crank out kids if they aren't able to provide for them. Humans could learn a lot from them.

The Snowy Owl fall migration is a complicated and poorly understood event. Most years, the majority of these birds remain north of the U.S. border. But some years, thousands of them leave Canada and spend the winter with us. It was once thought that low lemming populations caused the birds to push south looking for food. However, recent research has failed to back this up. More studies need to be done, but it's tough to find people who want to go out and study birds when it's eighty below. Apparently, even birders have a little common sense. Who knew?

This hasn't been a great year for seeing Snowy Owls, Rod, but if any place is going to get them, it's Syracuse. I sure hope you aren't the only person left in town who's alive. That would be lonely. Although repopulating an entire city could be kind of fun, if you know what I mean.

Doves Can Whistle without Moving Their Lips

Dear Bird Folks,
Nearly every time I walk out to fill my feeders, I accidently surprise a small flock of Mourning Doves, which, in turn, surprise me. When the doves take flight they make a high-pitched whistle. I'd like to know how they do this. Is it a vocalization or does the sound come from their wings?

—Simon, JEFFERSON, NH

I know what you mean, Simon,

We have a bird feeder outside one of the windows in our shop. Every morning, while still half asleep, I walk outside to fill this feeder. At least once a week I'm startled by a dove that bolts out of the feeder, zooming inches away from my face. You might think I'd be used to it by now, but I still jump and end up covered in birdseed. For the rest of the day I have to brush seed out my eyes and hair and shake it off my clothes. Even later that night, I still find bits of birdseed clinging to me when I crawl into bed. This doesn't please my wife as much as you might think.

With a population that ranges in the neighborhood of 350 million, Mourning Doves are one of North America's most abundant birds. I know many folks refer to them as "those stupid doves" (come on, admit it—you've said it) but the truth is they are an extremely adaptable and successful species. They can survive our frozen New England winters as well as the scorching heat of the desert Southwest. Interestingly, in some locations Mourning Doves are appreciated as songbirds, while in other places they are shot for fun. Each year hunters kill nearly twenty million Mourning Doves, more than all other game birds combined. Now you understand why the birds are always "mourning."

Most birds have an alarm call when danger approaches. We've all heard Blue Jays scream when the dreaded outdoor cat is spotted; crows do the same when they see a hawk. Doves can't do that. They don't have much of a vocal range. The only thing they can do is coo. Don't get me wrong; I have nothing against cooing, but it's not a great alarm. Try this: the next time there is an emergency, say, "Coooo, coooo." I doubt those around you will suspect there's trouble (although they may look at you funny). To make up for their lack of a strong voice, doves use their wings to announce danger.

When Mourning Doves take flight, air vibrates the tips of their flight feathers, which causes the whistling sound. This is not uncommon; most birds produce sounds when they fly. For example, wing sounds are what give hummingbirds their name. Conversely, many owls have had to evolve special feathers to keep their wings silent when hunting. What's special about the dove's wing sound is its ability to communicate danger; that's the theory, at least.

To test this theory, researchers recorded wing whistles of a flock of doves during both normal and panicked takeoffs. When they played the normal takeoff sounds to a group of doves, as well as to other birds at a feeder, none of the birds paid much attention. But when they played sounds of a panicked wing whistle, not only did the doves split but all the other birds did, too. It became clear that birds are able to pick up subtle differences between normal and panicked dove wing whistles.

The high-pitched whistles produced by Mourning Doves definitely come from their wings, Simon. These sounds are an effective way to announce danger and startle predators. While these wing sounds can be loud, they aren't nearly as loud as my wife can be when I accidently get birdseed in our bed. Some people are so uptight.

Cattle Egrets Fit Right In

Dear Bird Folks,
I've always been under the impression that herons and egrets are basically fish eaters. But on a recent trip to North Carolina, I saw fields filled with egrets, and there wasn't any water or fish within miles. What could they have been eating? Have egrets become vegetarians?

—*Meredith,* FAIRFIELD, CT

That's it, Meredith,

Egrets are now vegetarians. The thought of spearing little fish day after day has become unsettling to egrets. As a result, they have abandoned their barbaric ways, crawled out of the dingy swamps, and moved into open fields where they feed on wild, free-range tofu. By doing so the birds not only feel good about themselves, but their breath smells way better than it did when they ate fish all day, which really helps them in the dating world.

The birds you saw in the field are egrets, all right, but not your typical American egrets. They are Cattle Egrets. Cattle Egrets are one of the most amazing birds you are likely to see, especially in North Carolina. Seventy years ago no one had ever seen Cattle Egrets in North America; now their population may exceed all other herons and egrets combined. Originating in Africa, Cattle Egrets have been steadily expanding their range. First they moved into South America, then North America, and then Australia. They are like the old British Empire, determined to conquer the world. But unlike the Brits, these birds are actually welcome when they arrive and they want nothing to do with tea.

In the late 1800s a handful of thrill-seeking egrets somehow flew from Africa, across four thousand miles of Atlantic Ocean, to South America. Why they made such a blind-faith journey is anyone's guess. It could simply be they had extra air miles to use up or had a hankering for some fresh papaya. Whatever the reason, they apparently liked what they found because they not only stayed, but they thrived and slowly spread throughout much of the continent. When they finished exploring South America, the egrets once again became restless and in 1943 set their sights on North America.

Usually when a foreign species invades a new ecosystem, they become an annoyance (i.e., Japanese beetles, Norway rats, Mel Gibson), but this is not necessarily the case with Cattle Egrets. For the most part, they play nice and get along with the locals. Part of the reason why they have caused so few problems is their diet. They aren't big fish eaters and thus don't compete with the fish-loving native herons and egrets. As their name implies, Cattle Egrets are fond of cattle. However, they don't eat cattle. If they did, they'd be competing with us (well, some of us).

Cattle Egrets eat bugs. They are called "Cattle" Egrets because they are attracted to the insects the big animals stir up as they move about the fields. And if there are no cattle to be found, the birds are just as happy to follow a plow, tractor or even homeowners mowing their lawns. They are also big fans of brush fires. The birds feast on insects scurrying to escape the flames. Smoke from a fire attracts egrets from all over. It seems these birds don't often get a hot meal and they don't want to miss out.

Cattle Egrets are not vegetarians, Meredith. They eat plenty of meat, but it's mostly in the form of insects, the other white meat. Cattle Egrets aren't perfect. They can be a problem at airports and they occasionally start a smelly nesting colony too close to human habitation. But on the whole, they mind their own business and cause few annoyances . . . rare for a foreign species. Too bad we can't say the same about Mel Gibson.

Fearless Red-breasted Nuthatches

Dear Bird Folks,
We often have nuthatches in our yard. I know when they are around because I can hear their signature "yank, yank, yank" call. Today I heard what sounded like baby White-breasted Nuthatches, but after a closer look they turned out to be Red-breasted Nuthatches. I haven't seen them around here before. Are they new to the area, or have I not been paying attention?
—*Martin,* SANDWICH, MA

Come on, Martin,
I'm happy you saw your first Red-breasted Nuthatches, but I wish you had picked a different bird to ask about. I like Red-breasted Nuthatches as much as the next person but it's the name

I hate. Couldn't you have asked me about a Mallard or a Killdeer or some other bird with a shorter name? Why did you have to pick a name with twenty characters in it? That's a lot of extra typing. And don't get me started on the hyphen. My fingers aren't meant to type that little line. Every time I try to type a hyphen, I hit the equal sign, so the bird ends up being Red=breasted Nuthatches. The next time you ask a question, please consider me and my hyphen issues. I'd appreciate it.

Red=breasted Nuthatches are cute little birds, with "little" being the key word. They are smaller than chickadees and about half the size of a titmouse. They have gray backs, with black caps and distinctive white eye stripes. Ironically, what they don't have is a bright red breast. The male Rose=breasted Grosbeak truly has a red breast, but not this bird. Its breast is more of a soft rusty/orange wash. It fact, they originally wanted to call it the "Soft rusty/orange wash-breasted Nuthatch," but realized such a long name would have put me over the edge.

Red-breasted Nuthatches (hey, I typed it right!) can be found in southern New England every day of the year, but fall is the best time to look for them, and some falls are better than others. The vast majority of these birds breed in the northern United States and Canada, and many move south in the winter. Some winters we see few of them, but then there are years when it seems we are neck-deep in nuthatches.

Why so many? A mass migration is most likely caused by lack of food. Every couple of years the northern pinecone crop crashes, forcing the birds to head south in search of food. The influx of thousands of northern seed-eating birds creates great excitement for folks who watch birds and even greater excitement for those who sell birdseed. Migrating Red-breasted Nuthatches have had little exposure to bird feeders (or even humans, for that matter); yet, when they discover a bird feeder, they readily eat from it. Free food is, after all, free food.

Another oddity is that these birds love our feeders but hate our birdhouses. Even though they are cavity nesters, like chickadees and bluebirds, they rarely build a nest in anything they don't make themselves. They avoid birdhouses and instead hollow out a cavity in the trunk of a rotting tree. The female does most of the excavation, but the male is always close by to provide snacks and tell her what she is doing wrong.

A unique feature of a Red-breasted Nuthatch's home is that they cover the outside of the entrance hole with fresh, sticky tree sap. The birds carry globs of sap in their beaks and paint it around the entrance hole. No one is sure why, but it is believed it's an attempt to deter predators or the town tax assessor. Some fussy birds don't like getting sap on their beaks and apply it with a piece of bark. Really. This behavior clearly shows that these little nuthatches have the ability to use tools and that even birds can be annoyingly prissy.

Prissiness aside, Red-breasted Nuthatches aren't intimidated by any other feeding bird, no matter the size, and aren't afraid of one of nature's most sinister creatures, humans. The next time you see Red-breasted Nuthatches in your yard, walk up to them. They don't care. You may be a big deal in the world of people but you won't impress them in the least.

Red-breasted Nuthatches are fun birds to watch, Martin. They are energetic, friendly, and eat lots of birdseed. Gotta love a bird like that. If only I could get them to shorten their name.

Chickens Get No Respect

Dear Bird Folks,
My husband gave me a copy of your last book and, believe it or
not, I'm reading it and my bird IQ is soaring. However, there is
one question you didn't answer: Why aren't chickens pictured in

bird guides? I understand they are domesticated birds, but domes-
ticated ducks, geese, and turkeys are often in the books. Why not
chickens?

—*Carol,* BELLINGHAM, WA

You are one lucky lady, Carol,

I don't believe I've met your husband but I can tell right away he is smart. Of the millions of books out there, he chose *Why Don't Woodpeckers Get Headaches?* to give to you. That clearly shows he is a good husband and a brilliant gift giver. Either that or my book was in the sale rack and he's one of those cheap guys who can't pass up a bargain. Whatever the reason, it's all good—because you got a gift, your bird IQ is up, and I can shamelessly plug my last book. What could be better?

Domesticated chickens aren't in our bird books because wild chickens aren't native to the Americas. Conversely, we have both wild and domesticated geese, ducks, and turkeys walking around this continent. Including pictures of those birds in the books makes sense. You'd be surprised at how many people bring me pictures of a "mystery" duck or goose, convinced they have found some rare bird. They don't believe me when I tell them this rare bird has escaped from a pen. It's helpful when I'm able to point to a picture of their bird in a book. Domestic chickens, on the other hand, have no confusing wild American counterparts. If it looks like a chicken, it's a chicken. Any birder who needs a book to identify a chicken may want to consider a different hobby. No offense.

Some might argue that North America does indeed have native wild chickens. We have Lesser and Greater Prairie Chickens living in the plains states. Sorry, but they aren't true chickens. Prairie chickens are grouse and are chickens in name only. Just like cowbirds aren't bovines and catbirds aren't stupid cats.

To find truly wild chickens, you have to travel to the forests of southern Asia, where there are chickens as wild as any owl, heron, or Blue Jay. If you look in a book about the birds of India or Thailand, you will see pictures of chickens alongside all the other native birds. However, you won't see the name "chicken" under the bird's image. Wild chickens are called "junglefowl." The Red Junglefowl (along with possibly the Gray Junglefowl) is thought to be the source of all the world's domestic chickens. Junglefowl look very much like those dopey domesticated chickens we see scratching around a farm, except these wild birds are wary of humans and try to avoid us. The domesticated birds are easy to tell from the wild ones because they are typically very tame and often have those weird pop-up timers sticking of out them.

Researchers aren't exactly sure when man was able to domesticate the junglefowl, but it is thought to have happened around 5000–9000 BC. Domesticated junglefowl provided early man with meat and eggs for food, plus feathers for primitive pillows and ornamentation. Records indicate that the first person to popularize chickens for food was Asia's great Emperor Sanders. Few Westerners have heard of Emperor Sanders because he was a modest man who didn't like the title of Emperor; instead, he insisted his subjects call him "Colonel."

I should tell you where the name *chicken* came from. The problem is I don't know. You'll have to ask Emperor Sanders. However, I do know that wild chickens aren't the sissy birds the name *chicken* implies. The males are extremely aggressive and protective of the females, and will often fight to the death in their defense. In many Third World countries, the locals have taken note of the birds' aggressive behavior and have organized recreational cockfights. Cockfighting is illegal in the United States because it is considered cruel and inhumane. Instead, we force the birds into cramped cages until they become so fat they can hardly walk.

Then we hang them upside-down, cut off their heads, and serve them in a paper bucket. Our chickens are lucky they don't live in those barbaric Third World countries.

I'm glad you asked about chickens, Carol. No bird has benefited humans more; yet most of us give them little respect. The domesticated offspring of the lowly Red Junglefowl has proven to be a very successful species. On any given day there may be as many as 24,000,000,000 (that's right, twenty-four billion) chickens on earth. Wait! Change that number to 23,999,999,999. My carnivorous wife just walked in carrying a cardboard bucket.

Don't Be a Bird Bigot

Dear Bird Folks,

I live smack in the middle of the city. All around me are concrete and bricks. Last week I visited a friend in New Hampshire who has several bird feeders. I spent every morning watching an assortment of birds fly in and out for their breakfast. What a nice treat for a city boy. Unfortunately, my friend didn't seem to enjoy any of it. He was constantly banging on the window to scare away certain birds or other animals. He even talked about putting up an electric fence to "fry" the chipmunks and squirrels. I felt sorry that my friend couldn't enjoy his feeders the same way I did. Do all people who feed birds end up like my friend?

—*Ray,* SOUTH BOSTON, MA

Thanks, Ray,

I've wanted to write about this topic for years but nobody has ever asked, until now. Too many of the people I see every day are like your friend. We call them the "bird bigots." They claim to like birds but they only like birds that look and behave the way they think they should. We are talking ultra–control freaks here. They demand that only little birds come to the feeder (except for cardinals, which can do no wrong). They think big birds are evil and that squirrels eat from their feeders not to survive but to be spiteful. Spiteful? Squirrels are too smart to waste time being spiteful.

You would think that talking about birds all day would be a fun job, and sometimes it is. Other times I spend the day listening to whiners: "The crows wake me up." "The geese poop on my lawn." "The plovers are closing the beach." "The Blue Jays are talking about me behind my back." "The herons have skinnier legs than my wife does." It goes on and on. But nothing causes whining more than unwelcome birds coming to a bird feeder.

One day I got a call from a lady who wanted to know how to "get rid of" the catbirds. Catbirds? What could possibly be wrong with catbirds? I think even Dick Cheney likes catbirds. This lady was upset because catbirds were eating the jelly she put out for the orioles. I made the mistake of trying to encourage her to enjoy the catbirds as well. She angrily asked, "Is there someone there who knows something about birds?" I said, "Sure, lady, I'll pass the phone to someone else," and let her have a nice chat with Mr. Dial Tone.

I don't get it either, Ray. Where's the tolerance? Where's the appreciation for diversity? It would be somewhat understandable if we were talking about a group of toothless rednecks who enjoy shooting everything that moves. But the people I get complaints from, in theory, *like* birds. They put out bird feeders, yet hate many of the birds that come to eat. They scream, "The grackles are pigs." Come on. It's a bird feeder. Grackles are birds. The results should be obvious. It's like giving a party with an open bar and then complaining when people get drunk. As I said, the results should be obvious.

Don't get me wrong, I understand that birdseed costs money and that people who pay for it should have some say about who eats it. I get that. That's why some feeders are designed with specific birds in mind, or to keep out squirrels. Most of the time these feeders work great, but not always. That's just the way it goes. What I don't understand is the anger and the aggression. I've had people try to return feeders with bullet holes in them. I've had idiots who proudly tell me about squirrels, chipmunks, or raccoons they have trapped and drowned because the creatures were coming to the food they are offering. Nice, eh?

This column is supposed to be light, so I'm not going to get too preachy here, but I need to say that bird feeding isn't for everyone. If you are a mega-control freak who needs to bang on the window at the sight of a crow, or reach for a bazooka every time you see a squirrel, or put up electric fencing to "fry" wild creatures that come for your offerings, maybe this isn't the hobby for you. Sitting in front of a TV and playing the same movie over and over (so there are no changes, surprises, or adventures) might be a better choice.

No, not all people who have bird feeders end up like your friend. Most gaze out at their feeders, enjoy the variety of wildlife, and let the creatures sort things out for themselves. But like everything else in life, there are a few boneheads who want bird feeding to be something it's not—a rigid, predictable pastime. I feel sorry for those people.

Thanks again for your question, Ray. If you ever get to Cape Cod, I'll buy you an ice cream. But leave your friend in New Hampshire. He and the black flies deserve each other.

3.

A Few Things Even You Can Do

In the old days we used to try to attract birds by putting out hunks of stale white bread. Invariably, we ended up with starlings, sparrows, and the neighbor's beagle (dogs ran loose in the old days). Then one day someone realized that if we gave birds better options we wouldn't have to settle for starlings, sparrows, and beagles. In this chapter, we offer suggestions on how to attract such trophy birds as bluebirds, swallows, and orioles, even if you aren't from Baltimore.

The Cost of Running a Heated Birdbath

Dear Bird Folks,
I'd like to buy my husband a heater for his birdbath, but I'm worried it would increase our electric bill too much. Do you know how much they cost to run?

—*Rusty,* MILTON, MA

This may shock you, Rusty,

But I'm not an expert on electricity. All I know is, it's expensive and I hate it when the power's out. (Like I'm supposed to get out of the car and open my own garage door.) To answer your question, I had to do a little research. So I called my power company. I figured they would have all the answers about electricity. Right? Wrong. I spoke to a nice lady but she was clueless. Talking to her about electricity was like asking Donald Trump about hairstyle. I hung up and called my good friend Jeff. Everyone has at least one smart friend, and I'm lucky to have Jeff as mine. Two seconds after calling him I had all the info we need.

Offering water in the winter is a great way to attract birds. During winter freeze-ups I have a line of them waiting to use my heated birdbath. One cold winter's day a few years ago, a local woman brought in a photo of thirteen Eastern Bluebirds jamming into her heated birdbath. I love showing that picture to customers because it actually makes some of them gasp when they see it. People don't do nearly enough gasping these days.

I can't guarantee that a heated bath will make anyone gasp, Rusty, but I can guarantee that the neighborhood birds will be thrilled. Fresh water can be difficult for them to find in the winter. Sure, birds can eat ice or snow to get needed moisture, but swallowing hunks of ice on a frigid day has to rob them of precious warmth.

In addition to quenching their thirst, birds also need fresh water to keep clean. Remember, the only thing between a bird's skin and the elements is a thin layer of feathers. If those feathers aren't properly maintained, deadly hypothermia may result. Birds can't go an entire winter without a proper bath. Only my kids seem to be able to do that.

There are two ways of providing water for birds in the winter. One is to add a heater to an existing birdbath. However, those add-on heaters can be expensive to run, since they often use as much as two hundred watts of power. Also, if you lose power, your birdbath will freeze solid and may crack.

The better way is to buy a specially designed birdbath with a built-in heater. Most of these heated birdbaths, which cost nearly as much as the add-on heaters, are made of plastic and won't crack if they freeze. Since built-in heaters are sized for each specific bath, they often require less energy to run. Our most popular heated bath uses only fifty watts of electricity. Now you are thinking: "Fine, fifty watts is less than two hundred, but what does an additional fifty watts do to my electric bill?" This is where I needed help from my buddy Jeff. Remember him?

According to Jeff's calculations, which are based on Cape Cod's rip-off electric rates, using a fifty-watt heated birdbath will add roughly 24 cents to your daily electric bill. (I won't bother showing you the formula he used to come up with this answer because it makes my head hurt just looking at it.) Using a fifty-watt heated birdbath nonstop from December through March will cost you $29.04 for the entire year, or $29.28 if it's a leap year. So even during a leap year, the bath will cost less to use than some folks pay for a single bag of sunflower seed. But wait. It gets better. All but the cheapest heaters have built-in thermostats. That means they shut down and won't use any power on a warm day or during the January thaw. Thus, your bill could be even less than that $29.04, maybe $29.02. Sweet!

Of course, it would be great to have a way of keeping your birdbath ice-free without using any energy at all, but so far none of the solar products we've tested have done an adequate job. I've also heard of people adding treatments to the water to keep it from freezing. That's not a good idea. Never add anything to a birdbath that you wouldn't drink yourself. (Although my old man used to drink enough "treatment" to keep every birdbath in New England from freezing.)

I suggest you get a small birdbath with a built-in heater. It won't cost that much to run and your birds will love it. One more thing, Rusty. I don't know how much you like your husband, but if you actually do like him I suggest he plug his birdbath only into an outdoor outlet that has a GFI (ground fault interrupter). These outlets are designed to shut down instantly if something goes wrong, and will prevent your husband from getting a shock, or a permanent perm.

Clean Your Birdhouses!

Dear Bird Folks,
This spring our nest boxes produced several families of birds. We had a family of bluebirds, plus Tree Swallows, chickadees, titmice,

and nuthatches. Now that the babies have moved out, I'm wondering if I should clean out the boxes. Also, do you think any of these birds will try to raise a second family?

—*Charles,* BREWSTER, MA

So, it's you, Charles,

You're the one who's getting all the birds. A lot of people have been complaining that the birds aren't using the boxes I've sold them. Now I know why. All the birds are nesting in your yard. Your productive yard is making me look bad. I suggest you take your boxes down at once. If you don't do as I say, I may be forced to take action. One word from me, and your birdhouses would disappear. All I have to do is call my buddy "Whitey." Although Mr. Bulger hasn't been answering his phone lately. I hope nothing has happened to him.

I also like that you are concerned about cleaning your boxes. This is a very good idea. Birds appear to be sleek and clean, but they can be loaded with lice, mites, and sometimes cooties. These little pests may remain in the nest after the bird family has departed and transfer themselves onto the next batch of baby birds, often with unpleasant results. In addition, some old nests may contain rotten or broken eggs, or even a dead chick from the previous tenants. No bird wants to start a family with a rotting corpse in the nest. It's bad karma.

Here's another reason to regularly inspect your nest boxes. Last summer a pair of Tree Swallows attempted to build a nest in a birdhouse behind our store. I was thrilled. I was also surprised because the back of our shop is not really ideal breeding habitat for any creature, except maybe rats. Yet, between the dumpster, the asphalt parking lot, and customers lined up to complain about squirrels, a pair of swallows wanted to raise their family. Sadly, after checking out our box they moved on. Why? It turned out hornets had started to build a nest in that box and I hadn't noticed. Darn! I was so upset I couldn't talk, except to tell a new employee he had been awarded the title of "Official Hornet Nest Remover." (I love new employees.)

I recommend cleaning your boxes as soon the young birds have moved out. How do we know the birds have left? Watch for the lack of activity. When parents are feeding the kids they are in and out of the box every few minutes. When you no longer see any action around the nest the kids are probably gone. However, you won't know for sure until you open the box and look inside. Lots of folks are freaked out by the thought of "disturbing" a nest. Relax. Adult birds won't abandon their babies because you opened the box and stuck your big nose in it. And speaking of noses, don't believe the old wives' tale. The birds won't smell you, no matter how bad you stink.

The answer to your question about birds having a second brood is no, maybe, and probably. Nuthatches and Tree Swallows typically don't have a second brood, but chickadees and titmice occasionally do. The birds most likely to hatch out another family are bluebirds. Last week, a lady sent me a beautiful picture of a male bluebird feeding mealworms to his hungry kids. She also reported that while dad was busy with the fledglings, the female was getting the nest box ready for family number two. Bluebirds do a lot of breeding. Apparently, they aren't as innocent as they look.

Congrats on your fertile yard, Charles. I think having several nest boxes is the key to your success. Some cynics will say I encourage folks to put up more birdhouses so I can sell more birdhouses, but nothing could be further from the truth. I'm offended anyone would even think that. I encourage more birdhouses so birds will have more families and thus there will be more hungry birds around. More hungry birds means I'll sell more feeders and more birdseed. That's where the real money is.

Sugar Water Brings More Than Just Hummingbirds

Dear Bird Folks,

I've been feeding birds for a long time. In fact, I think I'm one of your top ten customers. Like many people, I now have orioles coming to my hummingbird feeder. Recently, however, a chickadee has been feeding on the hummingbird feeder, too. Is that normal?

—Nancy, HARWICH, MA

I'm not sure, Nancy,

I'm not sure if you are one of our top ten customers, but you should be. I like that you readily accepted chickadees coming to your hummingbird feeder and don't complain. Many folks enjoy whatever birds come to their feeders, while others are not so flexible. For example, I'd have a better chance of creating peace in the Middle East than trying to convince some customers that cardinals and Blue Jays are both interesting birds and should be enjoyed equally. In the world of bird feeding, discrimination is alive and well. I'm glad you aren't part of it.

The hobby of feeding birds is fairly new. Fifty years ago few people had bird feeders; of those, only a small percentage put out hummingbird feeders. Back then everyone was too focused on coonskin caps, hula-hoops, and bikinis. Fortunately for raccoons, those disgusting caps are out of style, and fortunately for the rest of us, the popularity of hula-hooping has slowed dramatically. (I won't comment on the bikini thing. I'm still sleeping on the couch after mentioning Vegas showgirls in another letter.) The point is, as more people put out hummingbird feeders, more species of birds will likely discover them. This brings up another question: Is it natural for birds to eat sugar? The answer to that seems to be yes.

Among the more common birds at hummingbird feeders, besides the hummers and the orioles, are the woodpeckers. When

I first heard about woodpeckers coming to sugar water feeders, I was surprised. It makes sense for orioles to be attracted to sugar water; after all, they love sweet fruit. But woodpeckers? Woodpeckers eat gaggy maggots and bitter bugs. Then it hit me. Sapsuckers, which are woodpeckers, live on sugar. They are sugar-eating champs. And sapsuckers don't just mooch off our feeders; they drill holes into trees and lap up the forthcoming sap. In essence, they make their own feeders . . . and I hate that. What would happen if all the birds started making their own feeders? People wouldn't need to buy them from me. I can't even think about it. Let's move on.

Naturally occurring sap attracts a surprisingly long list of birds. In addition to hummers, orioles and woodpeckers, some waxwings, warblers, mockingbirds, juncos, finches, and vireos also have a sweet tooth. According to you, Nancy, we can now add chickadees to the list. In nature, some of these birds satisfy their sugar lust by carefully watching the sapsuckers and then stealing their sap when they aren't looking. With other birds, sap taking is more serendipitous. For example, a broken tree branch may produce a flow of dripping sap that many birds will enjoy.

Speaking of saps, when I was in elementary school a spring ice storm damaged a number of sugar maples in my neighborhood. Hundreds of broken branches caused the trees to literally rain sap. This rare event not only attracted lots of birds, it also attracted me and several of my idiot friends. As we walked to school, we stopped under each tree and tried to catch the sticky drops with our tongues. We managed to snag lots of drops, but many more missed our tongues and splashed all over our faces. So what? We were having fun . . . until we got to school and the splattered sap began to dry. Within an hour my face had become stiff and rigid, and my hair stuck straight up. I looked like the love child of Joan Rivers and Don King.

Only a handful of birds have figured out that our humming-bird feeders offer sugar water, Nancy, but it's just a matter of time before other species of birds catch on. Someday we might see vireos and waxwings on our feeders. That would be cool . . . as long as they don't figure out how to make their own feeders. That would be not cool at all.

Bluebird Housing

Dear Bird Folks,

For the past several days I've had a pair of bluebirds checking out the birdhouse on my deck. They are there every morning. Some mornings they even bring bits of grass into the birdhouse. However, not long after they arrive they disappear and I don't see them again until the next morning. Where do they go for the rest of the day? Also, does the fact that they are putting grass into the box mean they are going to start laying eggs? If so, when?

—*Tina,* HARWICH, MA

Oh, brother, Tina,

I used to be jealous when people told me about bluebirds coming to their yards, but now I'm just annoyed. I've lived in the same house for the past two decades and have yet to see a bluebird within miles of the place. And you have them building a nest on your porch. What do you have that I don't? Maybe people should be writing to you for advice. How about this: "Ask the Bird Folks, plus Tina"? I should check with my agent, as soon as I get one.

Eastern Bluebirds remind me of my friends who went to private school. They are bright, well dressed, and charming but have few real-life skills. Bluebirds nest in holes in trees but don't have the ability to dig their own cavities. They are totally dependent on woodpeckers to excavate homes for them or for some retired guy to build them a birdhouse. Because the birds don't participate in their cavity's design, they must inspect several possibilities before deciding which location fits the bill. There's always a lot of checking and rechecking. Real estate agents hate having bluebirds for clients.

The first pairs of bluebirds to go house hunting each spring are most often older birds. While younger birds are wasting time flirting, courting, and texting, the veterans are getting down to business. It's the male's job to stake out a territory and find possible nesting sites. Typically, he'll land on the entrance hole of a cavity, shake his wings, and call to his mate. More often than not, the female rolls her eyes and says, "You're kidding, right?" As with most couples, it's the female who has the final say on choosing a home. And with bluebirds, the female deserves the right to choose. Not only will she be spending much of her time inside the new home, but the success of her family and her own life depend on her making the correct choice. She will spend hours in a tiny room with no back door or secondary way of escaping. If she chooses a site that is also attractive to local predators, in a short time she could go from being a mother to being lunch.

Eventually, the female will find a location or two to put on her "maybe" list. She usually brings some grasses or other nesting material into each site to see how they "fit" her. The decision process may take up to six weeks. In New England, bluebirds often start house hunting in March, but they are in no hurry. In case you haven't noticed, the weather in March can go from pleasant to ugly to mega-ugly in a matter of hours, and the birds know it. Laying eggs too early can lead to nest failures. But after many visits and a little price haggling, the female makes her choice and starts building her nest in earnest.

Once again, the female does most of the work. The handsome male bluebird is more like eye candy. He may carry a bit of material for her, but he really doesn't add much to the process. It usually takes about a week for the female to complete the nest. Most of the work takes place in the morning; the rest of the day the birds forage, preen, and catch up on their afternoon soaps.

Once the nest is completed, she may lay her eggs right away or she may wait. As I mentioned, if the weather isn't right or there doesn't appear to be a readily available food supply, she could delay egg laying. Keep that last bit in mind. If the birds suddenly stop coming to the box, there is no reason to think they have abandoned the nest, been eaten by a hawk, or run off to join a cult. There's a good chance the birds will return and start raising a family.

What I find interesting about your bluebirds, Tina, is that they are using a birdhouse on your porch. That's not their typical nesting habitat. I tell people that bluebirds like open areas. Also, their houses should be mounted on poles to help discourage predators, and the poles should be only about six feet high to allow for easy cleaning. Perhaps I don't know as much as I think. Maybe I'm like a male bluebird—just eye candy. I can live with that.

Tree Swallows, the Bluebird Alternative

Dear Bird Folks,
We have a large open yard and would like to put up some bird-houses to attract Tree Swallows. If we put up several houses, are we likely to get more than one pair?

—*Tim,* BRATTLEBORO, VT

Good idea, Tim,

I like that you are putting up houses for Tree Swallows. With bluebird mania sweeping the country, it's nice that at least a few people haven't forgotten about swallows. Tree Swallows are sweet birds and every bit as handsome as bluebirds. Plus, they'll eagerly come to manmade nest boxes and eat lots of annoying insects, and they're far more entertaining to watch. There are other good things to say about Tree Swallows, but I'd rather not do any more swallow-versus-bluebird comparisons. I don't want to upset the bluebird people. They're a rough crowd. With them it's all blue-birds or nothing.

As the name implies, trees are important to Tree Swallows. But the trees they covet are dead trees that have been used by woodpeckers. As is the case with bluebirds, Tree Swallows need a cavity in which to build their nests and, just like bluebirds, they have no carpentry skills. Woodpeckers, on the other hand, have enough skills for two birds. They hollow out their own nest cavity and once they're finished using it, they'll donate it to any bird that needs it with no compensation (although I hear they get some federal tax benefits).

Tree Swallows are fairly common summertime birds through-out much of North America. However, they are not typical back-yard birds, unless your backyard happens to be a farm or large field. But if you have a big open yard, you stand a good chance of getting these birds. Tree Swallows are gregarious and don't bother defending much of a territory. While they'll fight like rabid bad-gers to defend the nesting cavity they have claimed, it's fine with them if another swallow wants to live in the dead tree next door.

Another cool thing about Tree Swallows is they don't mind people. If there aren't any natural tree cavities available, they'll readily come to inexpensive bird boxes. The key word here is "inexpensive." You won't need one of those trophy homes that Purple Martins require, or to build a barn like Barn Swallows demand, or own a bank—mandatory if you want to attract Bank Swallows. Tree Swallows are simple folk, and a basic box is all they need.

Although Tree Swallows like their boxes plain on the outside, they prefer it fancier on the inside. In addition to the typical nesting material, Tree Swallows have a feather fetish. They love to line their nests with feathers, especially white feathers, and no one really knows why. Some researchers have suggested it has to do with camouflage or insulation. If Freud were a birder, he may have proposed that the birds harbor a latent desire to be swans. Whatever, Sigmund.

This feather thing might seem insignificant to us but the swallows are consumed by it. They will sometimes fly for miles to locate white feathers. Finding the right feathers is challenging enough but getting them back to the nest can be even more difficult. Neighboring swallows often try to steal feathers from a bird returning home, leading to dramatic aerial chases with the feather-carrying bird pursued by several others.

Once the chased bird makes it into its cavity the whole event should be over, but that's not always so. Sometimes the pursued bird reemerges from the cavity and continues to fly around with its prized feather, inviting other swallows to chase it again. And if the others have lost interest in the game, the bird will drop the feather in hopes of sparking their interest once more. It is similar to dogs that want you to toss a tennis ball to them, only with less drool.

I don't know how much land you have, Tim, but Tree Swallows really like to be out in the open. The farther you put your

nest boxes from living trees and buildings, the happier they'll be. Spacing boxes about thirty feet apart should be fine. I encourage people to put up lots of birdhouses, and it's not just because I sell birdhouses (although that has something to do with it). The more boxes you have, the more birds you're likely to attract. In addition to swallows and bluebirds, birds such as chickadees, titmice, and nuthatches use birdhouses. If you cheap out and only put up one box, you could end up with lots of birds squabbling and fighting, and there's enough of that in the world already. I'm talking to you, bluebird people.

Homeless Baby Ospreys

Dear Bird Folks,

For the past nine summers I have had the pleasure of watching a pair of Ospreys return to a nesting platform. Presently, the platform is home to two chicks, both of which are able to fly. The platform's owner has taken it down because it's in desperate need of repair. That's fine, but all I can hear are the cries of the young Ospreys searching for their missing nest. What will happen to these babies now that they are homeless?

—Leslie, NC

I'm glad, Leslie,

I know this whole thing is stressing you out, but I'm glad to hear the Osprey platform is being repaired. A few years ago I wrote a column that discouraged inexperienced people from putting up platforms. Soon after that I received an e-mail from a guy who was upset because he thought I should be encouraging more platforms, not fewer.

More *well-built and well-maintained* platforms are great, but the last thing the birds need is a platform that will collapse under the weight of a heavy nest or blow over in a storm. An entire breeding season can be lost if a nest comes tumbling down. Like bird feeders and birdhouses, nesting platforms have to be maintained or they'll be doing the birds more harm than good. That's my soapbox speech for today.

Right now, you are thinking: "Fine. Fix the darn platform, but does it have to happen while the birds are using it?" I have to admit it does seem like a bad idea to force any young birds off their nest, especially young Ospreys. Ospreys have huge separation issues and hate to leave home. Even after they can fly, young Ospreys, like their human counterparts, regularly return home to beg for food, sleep, do their laundry, and run up their parents' food bill.

Don't worry. While the platform is down, the baby birds will fly to a new location, most likely a nearby tree, where they'll yell for food. If the parents' ears are as good as yours, Leslie, they will hear their babies' begging calls (the "cries" you are hearing) and will keep feeding them. Once the platform is repaired, I'll bet the kids will come right back to it. From there they will continue to beg and the parents will continue to bring them freshly caught fish, and everyone will be happy (except the fish).

I understand why you might be concerned about the baby Ospreys, Leslie, especially after hearing their begging calls. But don't let these little con-birds fool you. At this stage they probably can take care of themselves but are too lazy. When some young Ospreys aren't given enough to eat, they don't catch their own food, but instead will fly to a nearby nest and beg from the family next door. Apparently adults can't tell their own kids from their neighbors' and will feed any bird that begs. Although it may seem as if the adult birds are being generous, they, like human adults, are simply doing whatever it takes to shut the kids up.

One more thing: As I was finishing this column, I received a second note from Leslie. She said the repairs to the platform were completed and, as I predicted, the young Ospreys have returned. I got something right this week. Guess I was due.

Vintage Birdseed Is Not the Best

Dear Bird Folks,

We just opened our summer home in Chatham. One of the first things I did was set out my bird feeders. Is the birdseed I stored in the closet last fall okay to use?

—*Paul,* RUTLAND (AND CHATHAM), MA

I like Rutland, Paul,

Rutland is the geographic center of Massachusetts. That means you can drive in any direction without having to cross a bridge (unlike Cape Cod). In Rutland, the only direction you have to worry about is southeast. If you head southeast, you end up in Worcester. That's not good. My relatives live in Worcester. Enough said.

I never suggest birdseed be stored for long periods. After being away for the winter, too many people return to find some furry creature has discovered a secret entrance into their closet and helped itself to the seed stash. In addition, unless the seed is kept cool, meal moth eggs, found in all seed, may hatch out and turn the seed into a webby mess. When either of those things happens, it somehow is my fault; I'm not sure why, but I've learned to accept it.

If the old seed hasn't been eaten, gone buggy, or gotten moldy (another thing I get blamed for), it's most likely safe to feed to the birds. However, that doesn't apply to thistle/nyjer seed. Those little seeds have a short shelf life and will dry out in a few months. Old thistle isn't harmful, but the birds will spit it out and hate you. When that happens, Paul, you know who gets the blame, don't you? For my sake, don't store seed over the winter.

Orioles Like It Sweet, Perhaps Too Sweet

Dear Bird Folks,
I hope to attract orioles this spring. I understand they also drink sweet syrup just like hummingbirds do. Is the formula for hummingbird food the same for orioles?

—*Kevin,* ROUND LAKE, NY

Yes, but, Kevin,

I say the two formulas are the same, but there are folks out there who will disagree with me. Can you imagine? I normally tell people to use the same formula for orioles that they use for hummingbirds (four parts water to one part sugar). I've read that a weaker mixture (six parts water to one part sugar) should be used for orioles. Using a bit less sugar will lower your sugar bill and help the orioles keep their slender figures. However, the number of customers who tell me they have orioles drinking from their hummingbird feeders suggests that orioles totally dig that four-to-one mixture. I say start with the sweeter mixture and, once you have the birds coming, you can cheap out and use less sugar. I won't tell the birds unless they ask.

While we're on the topic of orioles, I want to mention two other popular methods of attracting them. The tradition of putting out orange halves for orioles has been around since Florida invented oranges. Not only do the birds love them, but there is no need to buy a special feeder, thus no extra expense and nothing to clean.

Recently, people have started offering grape jelly. Orioles are jelly junkies; a small dish of grape jelly can be an oriole magnet. That's the good news. The bad news is that some people get sloppy with their jelly, which does the birds serious harm. Several wildlife rehabilitators told me nasty stories of orioles dying from exposure after their feathers became matted down with gooey jelly. If you offer jelly, place it in small dishes and fill and clean them regularly. Do not, as some boneheads have, put out an open jar of jelly. As the birds dip their heads inside to eat, their feathers come in contact with the sticky sides of the jar. Eventually, the birds end up looking like the cashier at Winn-Dixie who always uses way too much hairspray . . . only in this case it can be deadly.

It's important to note that May is prime time for attracting orioles. That is when thousands of hungry migrating orioles pass through and readily stop in our backyards if we offer them something. However, as May inevitably turns into June, the migration ends and the local orioles get down to the business of raising a family. Now insects become their food of choice. In June most people find they have fewer, if any, orioles at their feeders. If you haven't put out your oranges or feeders yet, you may have missed your best chance to attract them. Your next-best chance will be later in summer when the hungry baby birds are flying around.

I use the hummingbird formula, Kevin, but other folks use a weaker solution and that also seems to work. What's more important is that you do whatever it takes to keep the birds from getting sticky feathers. Life is tough enough for birds without making them look like that Winn-Dixie cashier.

Oh, Rats!

Dear Bird Folks,
My ninety-five-year-old mother has fed birds for years. I'm convinced her love of birds is what has kept her going this long. She recently moved into a nursing home where she was told bird feeders are not allowed. When I asked why, the people in charge told me they are afraid the feeders attract rats. Is that true? What can I say to make them change their minds?

—Tim, ELMIRA, NY

That's great news, Tim,

Not the part about your mom not being able to have bird feeders. That totally stinks. But I'm thrilled to learn that feeding birds has kept your mom alive and well for ninety-five years. Do you know what that means? I can stop all this silly exercising, drinking carrot juice, and eating low-fat ice cream. (Eating low-fat ice cream is like being dead already.) With all the bird feeders I have in my yard, I should live until at least 149, and maybe longer if my neighbor's cat doesn't put out a contract on me. (Snowball and I don't get along.)

But really, nobody should tell your ninety-five-year-old mother what she can and cannot do. At her age she shouldn't have to listen to anybody, except maybe a ninety-six year old. And if that ninety-six year old happens to be a man, she only has to pretend to listen.

I talk with hundreds of people every day, and rarely does anyone mention rats. (Actually, I don't mind hearing the occasional rat story. It's a nice break from the squirrel complaints.) Do rats eat birdseed? Of course, they do. Rats eat everything, except for maybe pimento loaf. What's up with that stuff?

But where are most rats found? (Don't say law school, that's too obvious.) Rats are found in big cities, and most big cities have very few bird feeders. It's our garbage and sloppy lifestyles that keep rats fat and happy, not bird feeders. If you want to see rats, don't look for a bird feeder; find a dumpster. Dumpsters, including the ones at nursing homes, are rat magnets.

Here are some suggestions you can present to the powers-that-be at your mother's new home. The best way to rat-proof a feeding station is to never use that awful "mixed seed." The birds will toss most of that crap on the ground, where who-knows-what creature will come along to clean it up. Instead, offer hulled sunflower seeds. The birds love it, there is no waste, and no empty shells on the ground.

You should also add a tray to every feeder. If a bird does drop a few seeds, they'll land in the tray, where another bird, usually a cardinal, will eat them. Tell the musophobes (rat phobics) that your feeders will also have squirrel baffles on them. Baffles will prevent any creature—including rats—from climbing up. With no seed on the ground and no way for anything to get onto the feeder, there will be no rats. (Just don't look in the dumpster.)

I have many customers who buy feeders and birdseed for relatives in nursing homes. Several of the facilities actually encourage bird feeding. Recently, I read about a place in Bellingham, Washington, that even advertised in the local paper for used feeders. After bingo and kickboxing, watching the birds was one of the seniors' favorite activities.

The idea of denying older people a bit of pleasure is really unsettling. They are not prisoners sentenced to the Rock. We're talking about aging folks who have had to give up their homes and their yards. They shouldn't be forced to give up their birds because some director watched *Willard* or *The Pied Piper* too many times.

Rats are rarely a problem at bird feeders and won't ever be one with a few precautions. Don't be afraid to show the bigwigs this column, Tim. Hopefully, it will change their minds. If that doesn't work, have them call me. Rats will be the least of their problems.

Rotating Seed

Dear Bird Folks,

I found your book on bird advice in our local library. I enjoyed reading it, but I have a question. On page 88 you advise us to remove all the old seed from our bird feeders each time we fill them. Then, after we add new seed, you said to put the old seed back on top. But since most tube-style bird feeders feed from the bottom, won't the fresh seed be eaten first while the old seed, now on the top, won't get eaten?

—*Irwin,* EMMONS, NY

Not the library, Irwin,

Stay away from those evil places. I don't know which disturbed individual came up with the idea of offering books people can read for free, but I can tell you it wasn't a starving author. We need people to buy books, not read them for nothing. Next you'll be telling me that you get your bird feeders from the Red Cross and your birdseed from the free clinic.

I'm kidding, of course. I'm flattered that a library would carry my book and I'm super flattered that someone would actually read it. However, I'm not kidding about the importance of keeping your birdseed fresh. If we make the effort to invite birds to our yards, we also need to ensure that the food we offer isn't spoiled. Don't make me go all Martha Stewart on you.

After rereading page 88, I discovered you left out a few details. My first suggestion is to completely empty your feeder each time you fill it. Never, ever, *ever* top it off. If the old seed looks wet, clumpy, and moldy, dump it in the trash, not on the ground. Moldy seed can be fatal to birds. If the old seed looks okay, then spread it on the ground for the sparrows and doves to eat. Ground-feeding birds enjoy eating, too, you know.

As an alternative to spreading old seed on the ground, I also suggest (and I'm not pointing fingers) that cheap people simply rotate their seed. Pour the old seed into a coffee can, add some new seed to the empty feeder and then finish filling it with the seed from the coffee can. Since getting your note, I'm now suggesting a third idea: if the old seed looks good, simply mix it in with the new seed. That way you won't have to worry about the old stuff being endlessly moved to the top. Good thinking, Irwin. I owe you a quarter.

What can be gained from remixing or rotating seed? Who needs the extra work? For one thing, rotating allows you to inspect the old seed to make sure it is still good. Also, most feeders aren't designed well and are often produced in a particular foreign country that can't figure out how to make safe baby formula and pet food, so you know their bird feeders are going to be sketchy. But even locally made feeders aren't perfect. Because of design flaws, too often pockets of seed get trapped at the bottom of the feeder where the birds can't reach them. If trapped seed isn't cleaned out regularly, it will rot and you know what one rotten seed will do to the whole bushel, or whatever that expression is.

Weather also creates problems for feeders. Last January I was filling my feeder and discovered a problem that's common in winter. Hearing my own nagging advice in my head, I tried to dump the old seed but it wouldn't come out. It was frozen solid from all the rain/ice we had. I brought the feeder into the kitchen, set it on the counter and decided to warm it up with a hair dryer. (It seemed like a good idea at the time.) The hair dryer warmed up the birdseed all right, but it also blew it all over the kitchen counter with most of it landing in my wife's bowl of granola. Fortunately, she had stepped out of the room and didn't see what happened. What she doesn't know won't hurt her, right?

The point of this domestic drama is if I had simply topped off the feeder instead of emptying it, the frozen seed would have blocked the new seed from flowing to the holes and the birds would have gone hungry. Another problem is that seed companies allow a certain percentage of debris in their bags of seed, usually in the form of twigs, shells, clumsy farmers' fingers, etc. The birds won't eat this debris and it slowly filters its way to the bottom, where it can also clog the holes.

I definitely recommend that you empty your feeders each time you fill them, Irwin. The cheap people should remix or rotate their seeds, but it's best if you spread the old seed on the ground for the sparrows. Or sprinkle it into your wife's granola. I won't tell.

4.

There's More to Life Than the Backyard

Now it's time to crank things up a notch. Let's leave the coziness of the backyard and discover birds that many people have never heard of and for the most part, don't care about. Still, it's my job to expand your birding horizons. Besides, if I'm forced to answer questions about longspurs and Pyrrhuloxias, the least you could do is glance at this section.

Pyrrhuloxia Is a Real Bird (Not a Strange Disease)

Dear Bird Folks,
A friend sent me a postcard from Arizona. The picture on the front of the card depicts several birds. One is a cardinal, but the caption reads "Pyrrhuloxia." I don't know a lot about birds, but I know what a cardinal looks like. Why did they call it a Pyrrhuloxia? Is that another name for a cardinal?

—*Dustin,* BERLIN, NH

It's not a cardinal, Dustin,

I know the bird on the front of your postcard looks like a cardinal, but it isn't. It's a Pyrrhuloxia, which is a real bird even if its name looks like a bad Scrabble hand. The Pyrrhuloxia is a cardinal wannabe, and who can blame it? Cardinals have a look that humans can't get enough of. As I mentioned in the letter "Swans Support Integration" (were you paying attention?), the Northern Cardinal is the state bird of seven states; two professional sports teams are named after it, and several colleges have it as their mascot. So, it makes sense that another bird would also want to look like a cardinal.

What I don't get is why the bird allows itself to be called a Pyrrhuloxia (which, in theory, is pronounced "pir-uh-LOK-see-uh," I guess). Talk about a bad career move. It's like a cookie trying to compete with Oreos by calling itself "Hydrox." I think if Pyrrhuloxias changed their name to something snazzy like, say, "Vegas Cardinals," it would totally transform their image.

How did the Pyrrhuloxia end up with such a scary-looking name? And what does Pyrrhuloxia mean? It's all Greek to me. Really, it is Greek. The Pyrrhuloxia's name comes from the combination of two Greek words: "flame," which has to do with the male's red breast, and "crooked," referring to its large beak.

Found in the desert southwest, Pyrrhuloxias typically like drier habitats than cardinals do. Because of this preference, some folks who can't pronounce Pyrrhuloxia simply refer to it as the "desert cardinal." That isn't bad, but Vegas Cardinal would be so much better. (Maybe I should copyright that name!)

Superficially, the Vegas Cardinal© looks like a female Northern Cardinal, Dustin, but here are a few key field marks to help with identification. Both birds have a crest, but the cardinal's crest has a ragged appearance; the Pyrrhuloxia's crest is smooth and tall, often sticking straight up, which makes the bird look like it's wearing a dunce hat (not that I would know what a dunce hat

looks like). Also, Pyrrhuloxias have a more curved culmen than cardinals. Having a deeply curved culmen may sound like something the birds should be embarrassed about, but the culmen is nothing more than the top portion of the beak. A sharp down-curved beak gives the Pyrrhuloxias a parrotier look. If you are too shy to measure the bird's culmen, a more obvious field mark is beak color. Northern Cardinals have a bright red-orange beak, whereas the Pyrrhuloxia's beak is yellow in the summer and dusky in the winter, but never red. (Joe McCarthy would approve.)

Pyrrhuloxias are typically found in parts of Arizona, New Mexico, and Texas. A good place to look for them is in mesquite thickets, where they use the plant's thorny branches as protection from predators. In addition, the birds eat the mesquite beans and use mesquite wood to flavor their steaks at the annual We Wish Were Cardinals Day barbeque. Unfortunately, cattle ranchers have cleared many of the mesquite trees, claiming the trees compete for the rangeland grass needed for the cattle. (That's what the birds get for eating steak.)

Although the loss of the mesquite has likely had a negative impact on the Pyrrhuloxias, these desert cardinals have also benefited from humans. As backyard bird feeding expands into the Southwest, Pyrrhuloxias are taking advantage of our generosity. Pyrrhuloxias and Northern Cardinals have even been seen eating side-by-side at feeders. Occasionally though, just to show its sense of superiority, the snooty cardinal will mumble something about the Pyrrhuloxias' deeply curved culmen and things turn ugly.

I don't blame you for being confused, Dustin. You can't be expected to know birds that live twenty-seven hundred miles from Berlin, New Hampshire. I also understand why you would question any bird with the name "Pyrrhuloxia" under it. It sure looks like the worst typo ever or an ointment you might use for a skin rash. But the Pyrrhuloxia is a real bird. It just has a lousy name.

Avocets, the Birds to See When You Can't Go Shopping

Dear Bird Folks,
I don't have a question, I'm just writing to tell you about a life bird I saw because your store was closed. One Sunday morning, on my way back to New Jersey, I stopped at your shop, but you weren't open yet. Rather than wait until 10:13 (your posted Sunday morning opening time), I did a little birding—and I'm glad I did. At the end of a road in Orleans, I spotted my first American Avocet. What a thrill. It made my entire trip. Thank you for not being open.

—*Gina,* MORRISTOWN, NJ

You're welcome, Gina,

I knew my laziness would pay off for somebody someday. Wait until my dad finds out that people like it that I'm such a slacker. Won't he be confused!

When I finally got to work on the Sunday in question, a friend had left an excited voice mail about the same bird. (It seems everybody—but me—gets up early.) You and my friend should be excited. The American Avocet is a rare bird in most of the Northeast. But unlike many rare birds that visit our area, this bird isn't some dull sparrow with no field marks; it's actually identifiable. The avocet is handsome, well marked, and a treat for anyone who sees one . . . even if it means missing a visit to my store.

If the American Avocet were human, it would be a supermodel. Its long, lanky legs go on forever. Its body is shapely and perfectly proportioned, while the neck is elegant and inviting. The long bill is thin and dainty, and the bird's coloring is striking without being cheap or gaudy. (Yo, peacocks, I'm talking to you.) The avocet is one bird that other birds would be jealous of . . . if birds wasted their time on such things.

The avocet isn't perfect, however. It spent so much time making itself look good it didn't bother to learn proper table manners. When the bird is hungry it leans its elegant body forward, dips its dainty bill into the water and begins thrashing its head back and forth, over and over, looking like one of my kids eating an ear of corn. By constantly sweeping its bill through the water and along the bottom, the bird is able to snap up small aquatic creatures it feels with its supersensitive bill.

Another unattractive thing about this attractive bird is its voice. Avocets have a piercing, high-pitched call that sounds like a combination of a spring peeper and a dog toy being stepped on by a fat guy. As you might expect, avocets use their call to communicate with each other, but they also use it to fool predators. It is believed the birds are able to increase and decrease the intensity of their calls; by doing so, would-be predators are unable to judge the bird's actual distance. This is especially true when avocets are on the attack. This pretty bird with the skinny legs is extremely aggressive when defending its young. When a predator approaches the nest the avocets may scream a warning or fake a broken wing, but usually they say, "Bring it on!" More than one predator has been whacked with the full force a flying supermodel.

The best place to see avocets in the winter is along the southern coast of the United States. They are often found in mixed flocks with another handsome shorebird, the Black-neck Stilt. In the spring the avocets migrate to our central western states to breed. The female lays the eggs and both adults take turns incubating. However, on the sizzling western nesting grounds the term "incubating" takes on a different meaning. Often the parents' most important job is keeping the eggs from overheating. The adults provide shade from the blazing sun and occasionally fly off, soak their breast feathers in water and return to cool the eggs with a summertime sponge bath.

Once upon a time, avocets nested in many eastern states, but (stop me if you've heard this before) overhunting took care of the eastern population. Audubon once wrote a beautiful description of an avocet colony nesting along a lake in Indiana. After he finished writing he put his pencil down, picked his gun up and wiped out the entire colony. Way to go, John James.

I'm glad you got to see a life bird, Gina. An American Avocet is a bird all of us should see at least once, and hopefully more than once. Just don't make a habit of leaving my shop before we open. There are enough names on the endangered species list. I don't need mine on it, too.

Spoonbills Don't Eat Soup or Chowder

Dear Bird Folks,
On a recent trip to Florida I stopped at Merritt Island National Wildlife Refuge and saw some great birds. What really caught my

eye were the Rufous Spoonbills. I spent quite a while watching those birds digging in the mud with their odd spoon-shaped bills. A spoon is great for digging mud, but how does the bird get its food? Does it actually eat mud?

—*Tara,* WILLIAMSBURG, VA

It's Roseate, Tara,

The bird you saw on Merritt Island was a Roseate, not a Rufous, Spoonbill. I believe Rufous Spoonbill was a jazz musician from Boca Raton. Rufous Spoonbill played the tenor sax, while the only sound a Roseate Spoonbill makes is a series of nonmusical grunts and squawks. For such stately birds, they are not pleasant to listen to at all. Yet I'd rather hear an entire family of squawking Roseate Spoonbills than listen to a minute of jazz. Sorry, Rufous.

The Roseate Spoonbill is a really freakish bird. You won't find another like it in all of North America. Even in South America, where they have tons of weirdo birds, you'll only find this one species of spoonbill. A quick look at the bird's bill and it's clear how it got its name and why few other birds wanted to copy it. The bird has a spoon growing out of its head. Who wants that? The only bird that was somewhat similar to a spoonbill was the Fork-faced Finch, and they are long extinct.

You'd think a bird as odd as a spoonbill would be well studied, but you would be wrong. Not much is known about the spoonbill's behavior. In North America, their range is limited to a few locations along our southern coast. Perhaps researchers don't want to travel to the hot, buggy, snake-filled spoonbill haunts, and I don't blame them. However, we do know a few things about spoonbills. One is that they don't eat mud or even mud pie (which I think is a mistake on their part).

If you've ever watched a flock of spoonbills feeding, you would notice that they forage by placing their bills into shallow water and then shaking their heads back and forth like they have one of Rufous's jazz songs stuck in their heads and are trying to get it out. As the birds slice their sensitive "spoons" through the water, they are hoping to come in contact with tiny passing shrimp or minnows. The instant prey is detected, the spoon snaps shut and lunch is served.

Having such sensitive bills and lightning-fast reflexes help the birds feed in murky water, which may make it seem like they are feeding on mud, but they aren't. In addition, they have excellent eyesight and can easily pluck fish out the water, heron-style. What's interesting about spoonbills is that, despite their apparent advantage, they rarely eat soup or even fish chowder. I know; I'm surprised, too.

During the dark days of the millenary trade, spoonbills were nearly wiped out by the dreaded plume hunters. For the most part, the hunters were after the white feathers of egrets, but since spoonbills often nested among egrets they were guilty by association. A few hunters, perhaps looking to justify the killing, made fans out of the spoonbills' wings, a swell use of one of nature's most unique creatures.

Years ago, a group of birders were observing a flock of spoonbills feeding in a quiet pond when a car drove up and some idiot jumped out and yelled, "Look! Flamingos!" What a bonehead that guy was. I felt bad for him. Okay, fine, I was that bonehead. I was much younger and a little excitable in those days, but it could happen to anybody.

At first glance one might confuse the Roseate Spoonbill with a flamingo. Both birds are a flaming pink color and inhabit similar habitat. But flamingos have those ridiculously long legs and neck, with a hooked beak that resembles a fat boomerang. Spoonbills, on the other hand, are smaller birds with white on their faces and necks, and, of course, their signature spoon-shaped bill. In addition, spoonbills are proud birds; unlike flamingos, they would never be an ornament on somebody's lawn.

As you mentioned, Tara, Merritt Island National Wildlife Refuge is a good place to see Roseate Spoonbills. In fact, it's a great place to see a lot of wading birds and waterfowl. There are numerous hiking trails, plus a seven-mile wildlife drive, which allows the casual bird watcher to see an assortment of birds without getting out of the car. A word of caution: If you take the wildlife drive and some idiot starts yelling about flamingos, roll up your windows, lock your doors and drive away. You don't want to get near that guy.

Kookaburras Always Get the Joke

Dear Bird Folks,
I'd like to see a kookaburra, the national bird of Australia. Are they only in Australia, or are they also found in countries that may be easier for me to get to?

—*Rick*, TORRANCE, CA

Now, Rick,

I'm not a guy who likes to point out other people's mistakes. Usually, I let it slide without comment. Wait, who am I kidding? I love pointing out mistakes. That is the main reason I chose to answer your question in the first place.

Here's the deal: Australia doesn't have a national bird. Unlike us with the Bald Eagle, the Australians opted not to play favorites. Like a mother, they love all their birds the same and haven't singled out one species as more special than another. However, that was not the case with the Australian Olympic Committee. They chose the kookaburra to be one of three mascots for the 2000

Summer Olympics. The other two were the platypus and something called an echidna. I'm not sure what that is, but I think it's some kind of body part. I'll look it up later.

Unfortunately, Rick, if you want to see a kookaburra, you're going to have to travel. There are four species of kookaburras in the world, and they're all in Australia, New Guinea, and an island between those two locations. A few kookaburras have been introduced to New Zealand, but if you are going to go through all the effort to see one, you should go where they are native. Don't get me wrong; New Zealand is a fine country, but it seems to have more sheep and rugby players than birds.

Kookaburras are actually kingfishers—terrestrial kingfishers, to be exact. They don't need to dive into water like our Belted Kingfisher. They are more of a forest bird and can live anywhere they can find food and tree cavities to nest in. The most famous of these terrestrial kingfishers is the Laughing Kookaburra. The Laughing Kookaburra is a contender for the world's largest kingfisher and my favorite. (I like a bird with a good sense of humor. There are so few of them.) Its diet consists of insects, lizards, and snakes, including poisonous snakes (that's a good bird). Unlike our Belted Kingfisher, which seems to hate everybody, the Laughing Kookaburra likes people and often hangs around humans looking for scraps of meat.

I once spent nearly an hour trying to sneak up on a kookaburra perched in a tree outside a restaurant. It was my first visit to Australia, and I was determined to get a good picture of this stately bird. Just as I was about to take the picture, the restaurant door opened and a customer walked out and tossed the bird a hunk of meat, which it snapped out of the air like a beagle grabbing a cookie. I had just spent an hour trying to get close to a bird that wouldn't have flown away if I poked it in the eye with my camera lens. Shows you what I know.

The Laughing Kookaburra's voice gives the bird its notoriety. Its loud, raucous call can be heard over great distances. The calls, which sound like "koo-koo-koo-koo-koo-kaa-kaa-kaa" (you can quote me on that), can be heard any time of day but most often at sunrise. The people of the Australian bush use them as kind of a poor man's alarm clock, or a poorer man's rooster. No one is sure how these laughing birds got their famous sense of humor, but it probably came from watching American politics.

Kookaburras appear to mate for life. That's a quality humans seem to find endearing, even though many of us have trouble doing it ourselves. They also have another human quality: kookaburras tend to stay in small family groups. During the nesting season the parent birds raise the young with the assistance of "helper" birds, usually brothers and sisters from previous years.

If you want to see kookaburras, Rick, you are going to have to make the long flight to the land Down Under. Even though they aren't the national bird, they certainly are interesting to see. And if you bring a hunk of meat with you, the kookaburras will be waiting for you at the airport. Just tell security the meat is a gift for the birds, and I'm sure they'll understand.

Lapland Longspurs, More Fun Than Going to the Dentist

Dear Bird Folks,
What do you know about the Lapland Longspur? I saw a beauti-
ful picture of one in a magazine while I was waiting in the den-
tist's office. Unfortunately, I was called in before I had a chance
to read the story that went with it. I'm hoping you might be able to
tell me something about it so I won't have to go back to the dentist.
—Kristina, HAMPTON, NH

No problem, Kris,

I'd hate to make someone go back to the dentist. The last time I went to the dentist I left my baseball hat there. When I went back to get it I told the receptionist I lost my "cap," and it cost me $1,200. I guess I should have been clearer.

Before we begin, I have a question. How many of you have ever seen a Lapland Longspur? Raise your hands. Leave them up so I can count. That's not many. Longspurs are one of North America's most abundant birds, yet many people haven't seen them. Some of us are spending too much time indoors, probably waiting for the dentist.

The name "Lapland" makes it sound like the bird should live way up in Scandinavia. Well, it does live in Scandinavia, North America, and Siberia, too, where it is called the "Lapland Bunting." Early North American naturalists used the name "longspur" in reference to the bird's extremely long hind toe. I bet if they were naming the bird today, "longspur" would be challenged. It may be politically incorrect to point out a bird's odd foot structure. Birds have feelings, too.

With its chestnut nape and solid black face, the breeding plumaged male Lapland Longspur is a striking bird. Unfortunately, we don't often get to see the bird in breeding plumage because it breeds way, way, *way* up north—past Hudson Bay, above the Arctic Circle, in some weird part of Canada called "Nunavut." Nunavut? Ever heard of that? Neither have I. Even my computer's spellchecker hasn't heard of it. Evidently, it's a new territory the Canadians forgot to tell me or my computer about.

Up in the vast, isolated area of Nunavut, longspurs breed by the millions. This area is so remote that longspurs are often the only songbirds to be found, and that's fine with them. The handsome, sparrow-like males arrive first, stake out a territory, and wait for the ladies. Because the Arctic nesting season is short, the longspurs don't have a drawn-out courtship. The male performs a quick flight-song display, the female says, "Yeah, whatever, let's do it," and the mating begins. Too bad all mating isn't that easy.

As soon as the nesting season ends, the longspurs pack up and head south to a more manageable latitude; in this case, the good old USA. Each fall millions of longspurs pour out of Canada, somehow avoid INS agents, and settle in for the winter. This raises the question, "If there are so many longspurs, why have so few of us ever seen them?" Well, longspurs like wide-open spaces; the vast majority winter in the middle of the country. Here, along the East Coast, we see comparatively few. Oh, well.

The other reason few of us see longspurs is because they aren't feeder birds. You aren't likely to find them in your backyard, unless your backyard is a hundred-acre farm or the Great Plains. In addition, come winter, longspurs lose their distinctive breeding plumage and look more sparrow-ish. Who has the patience to figure out sparrow-ish birds?

Longspurs are amazingly efficient at finding food. They can find a meal in areas where other birds would starve. Along the coast, they are usually seen foraging in the dunes, sometimes in the company of Horned Larks and Snow Buntings. In the Midwest, longspurs may be seen in huge flocks, picking up waste grains in farmers' fields. They are also attracted to fields that have been recently covered in manure. But who isn't attracted to that?

Let's review what we've learned today. Lapland Longspurs are abundant, sparrow-like birds that breed way up in a recently invented part of Canada. They like wide-open spaces and find food where few other birds can. Also, unlike you, Kris, longspurs never need to go to the dentist, which is good for dentists. It wouldn't be fun looking into the beak of a bird that just finished feeding in a field of fresh manure.

Caracara, the Mexican Eagle

Dear Bird Folks,

I recently moved to Austin, Texas, and am looking forward to seeing some new birds, especially a Crested Caracara. My Texas Peterson guide refers to them as the "Mexican Eagle," yet I'm under the impression that caracaras are scavengers. Wouldn't a better name for them be the "Mexican Vulture"?

—*Nathaniel,* AUSTIN, TX

Not me, Nate,

I'm not about to contradict anything Roger Tory Peterson has written. In the world of birding, his word is law. If RTP says caracaras are called "Mexican Eagles," that's the end of the conversation. If he wants to call goldfinches "flying lemons," that's what they are going to be called. In this case, however, I think Peterson is merely referring to the bird's colloquial name and not saying that caracaras are truly eagles. It's like calling Sylvester Stallone the "Italian Stallion." Nobody really thinks Stallone is a horse. Most folks think he's more of a horse's . . . never mind.

The Crested Caracara is a medium-sized bird of prey most often found in grasslands, prairies, and pastures. The vast majority live in Mexico and Central and South America. In the United States, they breed in Texas and southern Arizona. There's also a small, isolated population that breeds in central Florida.

Ornithologists don't quite know what to do with these unusual birds. About the size of a Red-tailed Hawk, they are too small to be eagles. But unlike most hawks, they love to eat dead, rotting things. So, as you said, Nate, that should make them vultures, right? Wrong. Ornithologists don't think caracaras are vultures, hawks, or eagles. For some reason, the folks in charge of such things think caracaras are falcons. Falcons? Are they kidding? Apparently, the researchers are spending too much time in the lab, breathing formaldehyde fumes.

Caracaras are beautifully marked with black bodies, white necks, red faces, and blue beaks. They are strong fliers, but not particularly fast. They have ridiculously long legs and are swift runners. (None of these traits sound very falcon-y to me.) The one thing they share with falcons is their love of meat. They'll eat meat fresh, rotting, or cooked.

Yes, cooked. Many birds of prey are attracted to wildfires so they can grab critters trying to escape the flames. But chasing down fleeing creatures is way too much work for caracaras. They'd rather sit back and wait for the fire to pass. After things have cooled a bit, they fly down to investigate the burned area, searching for any crispy critters that weren't quick enough to escape. To a caracara, brushfires are a giant barbeque. (Now I understand why they like Texas so much.)

When they can't find barbequed meat, they look for the next best thing—rotten meat. Every morning, long before the other birds of prey have gotten out of bed, caracaras search the roads for anything that didn't look both ways before crossing the night before. Like retired men combing the beach with metal detectors, caracaras are up at the crack of dawn, flying low, seeking fresh road kill. If they find a squashed squirrel or rabbit, breakfast is served. If they come across something big and tough, like a dead cow, they have to wait. Not having the tools to break through thick hide, the birds rely on some other creature—usually a vulture—to do the dirty work for them. Once the cow has been opened up, the caracara moves in and rewards the vulture by chasing it away.

Caracaras aren't completely lazy, however. They'll hunt if they are in the mood. Behaving like Cattle Egrets, they frequently follow tractors looking for insects or other creatures stirred up by the machinery. They regularly do their own stirring, too. Knowing delicious living things can be found under dried cow manure, the birds use their long legs to flip over cow patties in hopes of finding a yummy tidbit for lunch. This, of course, is another common Texas pastime.

Caracaras are often seen sitting on fence posts, dead trees, or on the ground. You aren't likely to see them soaring overhead like typical birds of prey because they are not typical birds of prey. Even their name is wacky. Many folks think they are named after Irene Cara, the singer from the movie *Flashdance.* It turns out "caracara" comes from the Guaraní, the native people of Paraguay. That last piece of information is supposedly true, but to be sure, you may want to check with some of your Guaraní friends.

So, caracaras aren't eagles or vultures; for some reason, they are falcons. Don't ask me why. I'm sure it has to do with their skeletal structure, DNA, or some other boring explanation. Whatever.

Good luck in Texas, Nate. I hope you see lots of new birds. If you get hungry, look for a brushfire or flip over some cow patties. You'll blend in with the locals in no time.

Not All Flycatchers Are Dull

Dear Bird Folks,
Recently you wrote about the differences between swallows and
flycatchers and stated that flycatchers are "dull-plumaged" birds.
I've just returned from southern Arizona, where I saw several Ver-
milion Flycatchers, bright-red birds that are not dull at all. I just
thought I'd point that out.

—David, SANDWICH, MA

Hold on, Davey,

Who are you, the Bird Folk Police, looking for the slightest flaw in an otherwise perfectly written composition? I appreciate that you read my column and have taken the time to write, but if you read the entire sentence, you'll notice I prefaced that statement about dull-plumaged flycatchers with the words, "with a few notable exceptions." I really did. Take a look. See?

Now I have a question for you: How could you go birding in Arizona in the middle of the scorching summer? Didn't the crippling heat bother you? Are you made of asbestos? I've been to Arizona in February, and even then it was too hot for me. After a few days of birding in the desert heat, I drove to Las Vegas because I've heard everything is cooler there. The rumors turned out to be true; everything was cooler in Vegas. Although I saw some showgirls who were pretty hot, but keep that between you and me.

Of the four-hundred-plus species of flycatchers found in the Americas, many are indeed rather plain. Only hardcore birders waste their time trying to sort out those bland birds. But, as you noted, the male Vermilion Flycatcher is one of the exceptions. Instead of blending into the background, this striking bird is so showy it would stand out in a busload of peacocks. Vermilion is the perfect name for it. The male is half black and half red-orange, and not regular red-orange. It's a shocking red-orange, making the flycatcher look like a cross between a Scarlet Tanager and a traffic cone.

The males use their flashy coloring to help attract a mate, but if that doesn't get the job done (though it should), they also have an impressive courting flight no lady could possibly resist. The males puff up their fluorescent feathers and float high above the treetops, appearing to move with the wind, almost butterfly-like. It's quite the show, nearly as good as the fan dancers in Vegas. Oh, right. I wasn't going to talk about them.

As is the case with many birds, female flycatchers are not nearly as colorful as their male counterparts. They are mostly boring brown. Some human females complain that it's not fair the male birds get all the color, while the females are often drab. But this inequity works out fine for the birds. Vermilion Flycatchers nest in fairly open areas. It would be nearly impossible to avoid detection if the females had the coloring of a traffic cone, but the dull coloring helps them remain hidden from roaming predators.

Vermilion Flycatchers aren't sociable birds. They tend to avoid other birds, including each other. If you see one, you've seen a lot. Ninety percent of their daily activities involve sitting alone waiting for food. Their feeding pattern is often described as "boomerang" style. They zip out, grab an insect, and seconds later are back in the same spot, like a boomerang, a very colorful boomerang.

The majority of these birds occupy a range that runs from Mexico through Central America all the way to Argentina. If you don't mind a little desert heat, there is a population of Vermilion Flycatchers that breeds in Texas, New Mexico, and Arizona, but the Arizona birds are required to carry identification with them at all times.

I'm glad you mentioned Vermilion Flycatchers, Dave. These vibrant birds are well worth writing about. I hope you know I was teasing about you being the "Bird Folk Police." It's nice to know people actually pay attention to what I write each week. A little criticism doesn't bother me. Just don't do it again or I won't tell you where to find the best Vegas showgirls (as if I actually know).

Nënë, Not Easy to Say and Impossible to Type

Dear Bird Folks,
I just returned from Hawaii, where I saw lots of new birds, including Hawaii's state bird, a type of goose they call "Nënë" (pronounced "nay-nay"). I would like to know where the name comes from. Does it mean something special in Hawaiian?
—*Mel,* TRURO, MA

This is a hard question, Mel,

Each week I spend countless hours working on answers to the questions I receive. First, there's lots of time spent doing research; then more time spent double- and triple-checking each fact, or something like that. But all that hard work is nothing compared to the effort I had to put into writing about Nënës.

Do you have any idea how long it took me to figure out how to write an *e* with two dots over it? On my computer I can communicate with people from all over the world, watch homemade videos of bulldogs on skateboards, or check my stock portfolio (if I had one). However, typing a double-dotted *e* is not easy. I pressed every button I could find, looked through book after book, and called every geeky person I knew before one of them finally told me the secret to the double-dotted *e*. What would we do without gëëks?

The Nënë, or Hawaiian Goose, is an interesting bird, but, except for the spelling, the origin of its name is nothing special. It gets its name from its call, which sounds to some folks as if it's saying, "nay, nay." That's it. Lots of birds, like Whip-poor-wills and bobwhites, have earned their common names based on the sounds they make. Nënës say their name, too. The problem is there is no letter *y* in the Hawaiian alphabet, so instead they put a few dots over the *e*. This explains why Nënë isn't "Naynay" and Hawaii isn't written "Hawhyee."

None of this letter talk should diminish your encounter with the Nënës, Mel. Seeing one is a rare treat, with "rare" being key. Not long ago the wild population was only around two dozen birds. Protection and captive breeding programs have increased this number to several hundred, which still isn't many. The Nënë's future is threatened by a host of problems, including illegal hunting, habitat changes, and three introduced mammals: rats, mongooses, and golfers. Like other geese, Nënës are attracted to golf courses, and more than a few of them have been struck and killed by stray golf balls. Apparently, there's no word for "fore" in Hawaiian.

Some reports suggest that today's Nënës are related to a wayward flock of Canada Geese, which somehow stumbled upon Hawaii 500,000 years ago. Enjoying the nice weather, fresh pineapple, and a steady supply of mai tais, the geese opted to stay. Another reason why these lost Canada Geese liked Hawaii so much is because, at the time, there were no land mammals to hassle them. With no raccoons, foxes, coyotes, or grizzlies to pounce on them, the birds became less attached to the protection of water and slowly became more terrestrial.

Over the centuries the Nënës' wings became shorter, their legs became stronger, their toes and toenails grew longer, and their feet became padded with less webbing between the toes. These adaptations not only helped them maneuver over Hawaii's rough terrain, but the geese also lost most of that silly waddle other waterfowl have to put up with. Without the waddle, the birds were no longer self-conscious about their gait. Now the only thing they are embarrassed about are those ridiculous Hawaiian shirts. Hopefully, evolution will eventually get rid of those, too.

Even though Nēnēs are rare and one of the most endangered geese in the world, they are not difficult to locate (once you get to Hawaii, that is). They often can be found close to visitor centers in Hawaii's national parks. Due to legal protection and captive breeding programs, Nēnēs are rather tame, approachable birds.

Also, as you said, Mel, the Nēnē is the state bird of Hawaii. It was voted that distinction in 1957. I mention this because Hawaii didn't become a state until 1959. I don't know how Hawaii had a state bird two years before it became a state, but I'm sure one of my smart friends knows the answer. Once again, thank goodness for gēēks.

5.

Bet You Didn't Know Birds Did This

We all know birds have feathers, lay eggs and can sleep standing on one leg. But you probably didn't know that some birds can fly the same day they crawl out of the egg, use echolocation to move about in total darkness, or fly under water. Then there are birds that eat stuff like paint, bees, and vinyl weather stripping. See what you've been missing? I'll bet your life feels empty now. Don't worry; I'm here for you.

All Hatched Out and Ready to Go

Dear Bird Folks,
I read that baby eagles can't fly until they are ten weeks old. I assume it's because they are so large. With that in mind, I'd like to know which bird is able to fly in the shortest amount of time after hatching. I'm betting on hummingbirds because they are so small. Right?

—Karla, WILMINGTON, DE

Wrong, Karla,

While your size-to-flight theory has some merit, humming-birds, like many birds, are born naked. That's a problem. The law clearly states that they can't leave the nest until they are completely feathered. Ever since Janet Jackson's infamous "wardrobe malfunction" at the 2004 Super Bowl, the federal government has forbidden nudism, even in birds. The only people who can see us naked now are doctors and the perverts at airport security.

It takes a baby Ruby-throated Hummingbird about eighteen days before it grows enough feathers to support flight. That's longer than some larger birds. A House Finch, for example, typically flies in sixteen days; a Song Sparrow's first flight takes only twelve days. Birds born with very few feathers are called "altricial." In addition to not having feathers, altricial birds are often blind at birth. (According to that same federal law, birds born naked must also be blind so they can't see each other's nakedness.)

Other birds, like ducks and quail, hatch out fully feathered and with perfect vision. These birds are called "precosial." Precosial birds have the ability to be up and on the move the day they are born. One other group of birds not only can see and walk right away, but can also fly from day one. These birds are called "superprecocial." I know superprecocial sounds like a name of one of the X-Men, but they are real birds. But being able to fly the day they are born is not what makes these birds interesting. What's interesting is how they are born.

Australia has three species of superprecocial birds, known as "mound-builders." Mound-builders have finally solved the age-old problem of raising children. They don't do it. In America we have our own avian slackers, cowbirds, which don't raise their own kids either; they trick some other sucker bird into doing it for them. However, these Aussie birds would never do that. Being Australian makes them far too polite to do something so devious.

Instead, they produce baby birds that are ready to go the day they pop out of the eggs. There is no parental incubating, no feeding, no flying lessons, and no lectures about running with scissors. Once the female lays her eggs, she is done with the entire process and never knowingly sees her offspring again. The mound does the work with a little help from the old man.

Here's what happens. The male mound-builder scrapes up a large pile of organic material, containing mostly soil and leaves. As the soil and leaves decay, they produce heat, which the male senses with his beak. The mound must be just the right temperature for him to breed. He won't mate if he has a cold mound, and who can blame him? If a female arrives before the mound is the correct temperature, she is driven away . . . but told to wait by the phone.

When the internal temperature of the mound reaches about ninety-four degrees, he's ready for her. The female lays about eighteen eggs, which she buries deep inside the mound. Then she is done and heads back into the bush alone. The male stays behind to monitor the temperature. If the mound gets too hot, he digs away some material; if it starts to cool, he adds a bit more. After about fifty days of mound incubation, the chicks hatch, dig themselves out of the mulch pile, and head off. There is no "Hello," "Good-bye," or "Thanks for the hot compost, Dad." The young birds just up and go. It seems a little cold, but at least the kids don't ask for money. So I'm sure Dad's fine with it.

One of the most common mound-builders in Australia is the brush-turkey. Brush-turkeys are not closely related to North America's Wild Turkeys, although both birds are principally ground dwellers and have freakish naked heads. Our turkey has the customary fanned tail, while the brush-turkey's tail fans laterally, sticking up like a fishtail or a rudder on a plane.

Because mound-builder chicks get no support from their parents, Karla, they have to be ready to travel right after they are born. Amazingly, they can walk, run, and even fly on day one. Yet it takes eighteen days before baby hummingbirds are strong enough to fly. That's what hummers get for eating so much sugar.

Some Birds Fly in the Dark Better Than Owls

Dear Bird Folks,
I read a story about bats and their ability to find food using echolocation. The article stated that some birds also use echolocation, but never mentioned which ones. That's where you come in. Do you know what birds use echolocation to find food?
—*Russell,* FREDERICTON, NEW BRUNSWICK

None, Russell,
No birds use echolocation to find food. That was easy.

What other questions do you have? Don't ask me the one about a train leaving Chicago at two o'clock, traveling at 100 mph, while another train leaves New York at three, at a speed of blah, blah, blah . . . What was the point of that question? Does anyone really need to know that stuff?

Okay, back to the birds. There are birds that use echolocation, Russell, but none of them use echolocation to find food. They use it to find their way home. Of the roughly ten thousand different species of birds in the world, only a handful have the adaptations needed to fly around in total darkness; surprisingly, none of them are owls. These few birds have one thing in common: they live in deep, dark caves and use echolocation to get back to their nests, not to obtain food. In the Americas, we have only one bird with that ability, and that's the super-strange Oilbird of South America. Yes, there really is an "Oilbird," and there is no other bird like it in the world.

Oilbirds look a bit like and are related to Whip-poor-wills. Both birds are nocturnal, but the Whip-poor-wills are totally insectivores, while the non-meat-eating Oilbirds eat fruit. (I'll take fresh fruit over icky bugs any day.) However, the birds pay a price for their fruit fetish. Their babies grow very slowly. It takes several months for young Oilbirds to grow on their produce-only diet. By comparison, the insect-fed Whip-poor-will babies are up and flying a measly sixteen days after hatching.

If Oilbirds nested on the ground, as Whip-poor-wills do, their slow-growing babies would most likely become a meal for some passing predator. To keep their kids out of the food chain, the Oilbirds, according to one theory, have opted to build their nests deep inside caves. In the caves, the only things they have to deal with are stalactites, trolls, and the occasional spelunker. Oh, they have to deal with total darkness, too.

After a night of fruit foraging, the adult Oilbirds return to their cave and begin emitting clicking sounds. Like a bat or a submarine's sonar, the birds use the clicks to help them fly through the cave and avoid the stalactites and spelunkers. The impressive thing is that Oilbirds don't have tiny, easy-to-maneuver bat bodies; they are big, crow-sized birds with three-foot wingspans. Not only is an Oilbird able to make its way through the cave's twists and turns in total darkness, but it can somehow find its own nest among all the other Oilbird nests. I can't find my TV remote in broad daylight, yet they can find their own nest in total darkness. I'm impressed.

The Oilbirds' clicks may help them find their way home, but they don't help them find a meal. Owls find prey at night by using their superb vision and hearing, which allow them to hear faint mammal squeaks or spot movement. Unfortunately, Oilbirds can't do that because fruit is typically quiet and rarely moves. The Oilbirds use a sense not employed by many birds—their sense of smell. Some fruits that Oilbirds eat are extremely fragrant; it is thought they can locate the food by following the aroma.

How did the Oilbird get its name? I'm warning you that the answer is a little gruesome. If you are squeamish, you may want to flip to another page or cover your eyes while you read. They are called Oilbirds because the young birds are filled with oil. Well, sort of. After months of a nonstop diet of tropical fruit, especially palm oil fruit, combined with zero exercise (kids never learn), the baby birds are way overweight. In fact, they weigh 50 percent more than their parents, and most of that weight is fat. Indigenous people often stole the tubby babies, boiled them down and used the oil for cooking and fueling lamps. See? I told you to cover your eyes while you read.

That's the story behind Oilbirds and their echolocation skills, Russell. If you ever want to try echolocating on your own, do this: The next time you get up at night, don't turn on a light. Make clicking sounds instead as you move around the room and see how far you get before you stub your toe . . . or your wife throws something at you.

Paint-Eating Jays

Dear Bird Folks,
This might be the strangest question you've ever had. In the past week Blue Jays have been coming to my deck, pounding on the railing with their beaks, peeling off paint, and eating the chips! Do you have any idea why?

—*Nina,* BREWSTER, MA

Not even close, Nina,
You may think paint-eating Blue Jays would be high on my list of strange questions, but it doesn't even make the top ten. Don't forget, in the summer we see a lot of people from New Jersey. Last year a guy from Paterson wanted to know where he could

see a "new thatch." What? He repeated it and gave me a look that suggested I didn't know much about birds. I handed him a bird book and told him to point out a "new thatch." He opened the book and showed me the bird he was talking about. It was a White-breasted Nuthatch. Apparently nuthatch is pronounced "nu thatch" in Paterson.

After receiving your note I started wondering what makes paint so delicious. Kids like to eat paint so much the manufacturers have to make it without adding lead. Dogs seem to like it, too. Painted doorjambs are one of their favorite things to chew on. And now, according to you, Blue Jays also dine on paint.

To find out what this paint-eating craze is all about, I went to my local Sherwin-Williams store and found the answer on the paint charts. The names of many of the paints are so yummy-sounding I was tempted to take a bite myself. Here are a few flavors—I mean colors—that I found (and I swear I'm not making a single one up): French Roast, Black Bean, Fabulous Grape, Wild Currant, Saffron Thread, Malted Milk, and Sunflower, which I suspect is the jays' favorite. The color that made me smile was a non-food-sounding paint simply called "Reddish." The paint namers were clearly in a hurry to get home the day they came up with Reddish. Talk about phoning it in.

Even though paint-eating Blue Jays are rare, they're not unheard of either. A few years ago the eggheads at Cornell's Lab of Ornithology looked into this subject. It turns out some types of paint contain limestone. The jays ingest the limestone-laced paint because limestone is a good source of calcium. The more calcium they eat, the less likely they are to break a hip, plus they won't have to blow all their cash buying Boniva from Sally Field. In addition to hip health, the females need increased amounts of calcium to help with egg production during the breeding season. Normally, the birds obtain enough calcium through their diet and the grit they pick up from the ground. But some years, the ground is covered by snow and ice, so the birds have to switch to plan B, which means eating paint.

One way we can help the Blue Jays, and save our decks and homes from being stripped clean, is to provide the birds with some calcium by putting out eggshells. While feeding one bird the shells of another bird's babies may be a moral dilemma for some people, jays have no problem with it. After you've made your famous rhu-barb and rutabaga quiche, take the empty eggshells, place them on a cookie sheet, pop them into a 250-degree oven, and bake the shells for twenty minutes, or until the edges turn brown. This kills any bacteria and gets rid of the gross, juicy stuff. Finally, crush the shells into small pieces and place them on a board, plastic plate or your grandmother's sterling silver crushed-eggshell platter. Put the shells outside, and the birds will take it from there.

Paint-eating Blue Jays seem to be most common in New Eng-land, Nina. A possible reason for this is the calcium in our soil has been depleted by acid rain. No one knows why this behavior is confined to just Blue Jays, though, since all birds need calcium. With that last sentence in mind, putting out crushed eggshells is not a bad idea. Many species of birds will be happy to take them, particularly when they are nesting. If you are lucky, you may even attract a few White-breasted New Thatches.

Bee-Eating Birds

Dear Bird Folks,
You recently wrote about bees at hummingbird feeders. That got me wondering if there are birds that actually eat bees, or are bees just too dangerous for birds to deal with?

— *Luke,* CUMBERLAND, RI

Luuuuuke,

I don't know why some people, including me, feel the need to pronounce your name like that, but I think it comes from the Bible. I seem to remember a passage that mentioned that every time Luke got up to talk about the Gospel, both Matthew and Mark would chant from the back of the room, "Luuuuuke," and the name stuck. Check it out. You'll see I'm right.

Like us, most birds have a healthy respect for bees. Birds can usually avoid bees and don't like to challenge them. One sting can be fatal. But, believe it or not, bees are nutritious and good eating. Few things in nature aren't on some creature's diet. Even stinky skunks and pointy porcupines find themselves on the menu of both owls and fishers. The same thing is true with bees. Eastern Kingbirds and Summer Tanagers will go out of their way to feed on bees. Yes, *out of their way*.

I'm not surprised that kingbirds eat bees; they are both fearless and crazy. While kingbirds are fearless (and crazy), they aren't stupid. When consuming bees, they apparently have the ability to select only the drones. What are drones, you ask? Drones are honeybees without stingers. How would you like to be a stingerless bee? Talk about getting the short end of the evolutionary stick. It's like being a quill-less porcupine or a skunk that smells like bacon.

Summer Tanagers are not as selective. They will capture any bee or wasp, stinger or no stinger. Tanagers hunt by sitting on a perch and waiting. When it spots a bee, it darts out, snags it out of the air, flies back to its perch, and beats it senseless. When the bee is dead, the bird removes the dangerous stinger by swiping it back and forth on the branch. Once the stinger is out, down the hatch goes the bee.

As the name implies, Summer Tanagers are typically only with us during the warmer months. With the exception of a few individuals, most Summer Tanagers leave the United States in the fall to live in the sunny tropics. The male tanagers are totally eye-catching, bright red from head to tail. They look like tourists at the beach who forgot to use sunscreen. The females, on the other hand, are greenish yellow, with no red on them at all. (Apparently, the females are smart enough to use sunscreen.) Both sexes have long beaks, much longer than their cousin, the Scarlet Tanager. It is thought the longer beak is needed to keep the bee and its nasty stinger a safe distance from the bird's face. Makes sense to me.

Don't expect to see many Summer Tanagers in Cumberland, Luke. They are rare birds in the Northeast, normally seen only during migration. The majority breed south of the Mason-Dixon Line. I don't really know where that is, so maybe I'd better just say they breed south of Hershey, Pennsylvania. I definitely know where Hershey is. Any town that specializes in Kisses is permanently programmed in my GPS.

Puffins Aren't That Fussy

Dear Bird Folks,

Puffins are often pictured holding a mouthful of fish. The heads and tails of the fish hang out of one side of the beak or the other. My husband claims the birds alternate the way they hang fishes' heads and tails from their beaks. Is this true? This may sound like a stupid question, but this argument has been raging in our house for years.

—Donna, BOXBOROUGH, MA

Good work, Donna,

You may have found the exception to that old adage, "There is no such thing as a stupid question." Let me get this straight. Your husband thinks puffins have a touch of OCD and will only carry fish in their mouths if they are somehow able to coordinate

which way the fishes' heads and tails are facing? Maybe I should introduce your husband to my wife. She once told me the same thing. I don't know about your husband, but my wife is normally pretty clear-thinking. I've only known her to do two unintelligent things: believing this puffin/fish head story, and marrying me. People still shake their heads over that one.

I'm glad you asked about puffins, because they seem to be a forgotten bird. Thirty years ago, when puffin populations were struggling, they were the cover birds on every birding magazine and were constantly featured on nature shows. Today it's hard to find a single story on puffins, unless you happen to cross into Maine, where the puffin craze continues unabated. Maine has a right to be excited about Atlantic Puffins, since it is the only state where the birds nest. The local shops sell everything from puffin candy to puffin hats to puffin underwear. That last item surprises me. When did people in Maine start wearing underwear?

Members of the auk family, puffins are black and white sea-birds with amazingly colorful faces, looking like nuns riding on a Carnival float in Rio. The best places to see puffins are in their breeding colonies, which can be found on both sides of the North Atlantic. England, Ireland, and Iceland have colonies, as do the Canadian Maritimes and the aforementioned Maine.

Unfortunately for us, most colonies are on isolated islands, which aren't readily accessible. But if you happen to take a spring-time trip to Ireland, swing by the Cliffs of Moher, which rise over seven hundred feet above the Atlantic and are home to hundreds of nesting puffins. The cliffs are also one of the few places where puffins may be seen from land. That means people like me can see the birds without having to deal with a rocking, seasickness-inducing boat ride. The views from the cliffs are spectacular, especially if it's a clear day, which has never happened in Ireland.

A puffin's nest is typically found in a rock crevice or a burrow the birds dig out with their massive beaks. The female lays one egg, never more, just like the Raven says. Once the chick hatches, both parents keep busy by bringing it a steady supply of fresh fish. This is when we see adult puffins standing in the classic pose, with fish dripping out of both sides of their beaks . . . in whatever position they were caught with no rearranging to alternate heads and tails. (Sorry, hubby dude.)

What is fascinating, however, is that the birds are somehow able to catch fish after fish without any escaping from their beaks. Puffins have evolved several adaptations that help them gather fish. The edges of the birds' beaks have backward-facing barbs on them. Their tongues have barbs, too. When a fish is caught, it is locked onto the beak barbs and held tight with the tongue. This allows the birds to continue grabbing fish, regardless of which way the heads are facing.

I hope this settles the raging argument you are having at home, Donna. Puffins don't have time to worry about fish-head direction. Their only concern is survival, catching enough food for their chicks, and getting a good spot on a Carnival float in Rio.

Kissing Cardinals

Dear Bird Folks,

We have a pair of courting cardinals in our yard. The male will hop over to the female, gently take her beak in his own and hold it there for a few moments. From what I can tell he is not feeding her but simply offering affection. We have been taught that birds' behavior is totally instinctive, but it appears to me that my birds are actually necking. Please advise.

—Sandy, ORLEANS, MA

Oh, man, Sandy,

I hate these kinds of questions. No matter what I say, I'm going to upset somebody. I know, I usually upset somebody anytime I write something. But this is one of those topics that really puts people over the edge. Half the people want to believe mated birds are really in love with each other. That group includes you and the French guy who made that mushy *March of the Penguins* movie. The other half of the population feels that love is strictly a human trait. That group includes many researchers, scientists, and Spock. The third half of the populace doesn't spend time thinking about such things. Those people are taking the right approach.

If there were an award for being the perfect bird couple, cardinal pairs would most certainly be nominated. Since they often remain in the same territory their entire lives, it means the cardinals you saw clinging to your feeder during a blizzard in January are likely the same birds building a nest in your cedar tree in May.

In addition, the male and female cardinals are sexually dimorphic. That doesn't imply they are kinky; it means the plumage of each sex is distinctive. When we see a cardinal couple, we can be certain one bird is female and one is male. This is not the case with many other bird couples, however. For example, Mute Swan pairs often remain together for years, but since both sexes look the same we can't be sure if the couple is made up of one male and one female or if they are members of the Don't Ask, Don't Tell Club.

Another cool thing about cardinal couples is that they have a progressive relationship. With most songbirds it's the male's job to do all the singing. He gets up early and sings as loud as he can to announce his territory, while the female stays at home putting on her face. Cardinals don't follow this rule. The females are excellent singers and can match whatever the males sing. Married couples often sing as a duet, making them the Captain & Tennille of the bird world.

All the extra singing apparently causes the female to work up an appetite because she insists the male bring her food as part of the courting process. Mate feeding is a common ritual among birds—and among humans, for that matter (a good meal can lead to a great night). But Mrs. Cardinal is rather demanding. By quivering her wings, baby-bird style, the female will entice the male into giving her food, sometimes as frequently as once every fifteen seconds.

It is thought that mate feeding helps with pair bonding, but there may be more to it than that. Some believe the female could be trying to gauge what kind of provider the male is. If he brings her a steady supply of seeds and worms, he's a keeper. However, if the best he can find are bits of Doritos and Slim Jims, she'll probably dump him . . . unless she happens to be from certain parts of the South. Then he'd be the perfect mate.

Some folks interpret mate feeding as a form of kissing. That's understandable because that's what it looks like. But if you think about it, passing food beak-to-beak is the only way birds can feed each other. They don't have hands and can't possibly afford silverware. Another thing to consider is that there are thousands of different bird species, each with its own weird courtship rituals. Most don't look very romantic by our standards. Have you ever seen a fat, spastic tom turkey strut his stuff? He looks less like Rudolph Valentino and more like he has a neurological disorder. Yet it works for him.

I'm pretty sure what you saw was mate feeding. I know you said you didn't see any food being passed, Sandy, but either you couldn't see the food or the male was simply going through the motions in an effort to fool the female into thinking he had food for her. If that's the case, he's making a big mistake. She may decide he is not a good provider and he could end up spending the summer alone, listening to Captain & Tennille records. That will teach him.

Hummingbirds—They're on Everyone's Menu

Dear Bird Folks,
I'm amazed at the flying ability of hummingbirds. Their flight speed and maneuvering skills must give them a huge advantage at gathering food and avoiding potential enemies. Do predators even bother trying to eat them?

—*BB*, MARSTONS MILLS, MA

You should have noticed, BB,

While you were noticing the hummingbird's flying ability you should have also noticed its size, which is very, very small. In the world of nature, the list of potential enemies typically increases as body size decreases. For example, mice are on just about every predator's menu, while a much larger mammal, like say, a groundhog, only has to worry about really big creatures like bears, bobcats, coyotes, and those weirdoes in Punxsutawney.

Small creatures, with little or no defenses, have to evolve ways to ensure their survival or their species won't last long. In the case of mice and doves, their ability to quickly breed new replacements is what works best for them. The tiny hummingbirds aren't necessarily prolific breeders but they do have those amazing flying skills you referred to earlier. And it's a good thing they have those skills because their enemy list is long, and at times hard to believe.

Near the top of a hummingbird's hard-to-believe predator list is, of all things, an insect. It's difficult to imagine that an insect can stalk, capture and eat a live, healthy adult bird but it's true. I'm not talking about some kind of giant, sci-fi super bug from the Amazon Basin. This insect is so common that everyone reading this column has probably had one living in their yard or maybe even inside their house.

Any guesses about what this common, but ferocious, insect is? (No, not a greenhead fly, but that's an excellent guess.) This hummingbird-eating insect is a praying mantis. Just like hummingbirds, mantises are attracted to both flowers and hummingbird feeders. However, the mantises aren't looking for nectar. They hang out near flowers or feeders waiting for other insects to pass by. Using their branch-like camouflage and lightning-quick strikes, mantises can easily snag a passing insect. If a careless hummingbird happens to come along, it will snag and eat that, too.

Spiders are another surprise problem for hummingbirds. The trouble is, hummingbirds depend on spiders for housing. Hummingbirds use snippets of spider web silk to hold their nests together. If, while they are stealing the snippets, the hummingbirds see tiny insects stuck on the web, they help themselves to those, too. However, like most burglars, hummingbirds sometimes get into trouble. Perhaps it's inexperience, or a sudden gust of wind, or too much partying the night before, but occasionally a hummingbird finds itself tangled in the web. Once entangled the tiny bird can't get away, at which point the resident spider moves in and . . . well, you know.

Next on the list of surprising animals that feed on hummingbirds are fish. Hummers will sometimes hover above the water's surface to catch bugs, with little knowledge of what lies below. At least one observer has reported seeing a bass leap out of the water and snag itself a fresh hummer for lunch. Frogs, toads, and even dragonflies are other creatures that have been known to chow down the occasional careless hummingbird. Then there are avian predators. Jays, roadrunners, flycatchers, and, of course, hawks and owls are happy to put hummers on the menu . . . if they can catch them.

You were right, BB, when you suggested that the hummingbirds' flying skills can get them out of trouble because they usually do. Most of the above events are fairly rare, and the predators we've discussed have little impact on the hummingbird population. However, there is one creature that really is a problem for hummingbirds: the dreaded out-of-the-house housecat. Uncontrolled domestic cats are an enormous problem for all small birds, and hummingbirds are no different. Even the hummer's flying abilities haven't evolved enough to deal with this non-native menace. It's too bad cats won't leave the birds alone and eat greenhead flies instead. If they did, perhaps I'd even like them. Maybe. Nah, probably not.

Vinyl-Eating Vultures

Dear Bird Folks,
This sounds unbelievable, but every morning several Turkey Vultures land on my back deck. They peck at my sliding door, ripping

the screen and pulling off the rubber gasket. I've called several places, but no one believes me. Do you believe me? Do you have any advice? Besides the damage to my house, these huge vultures are starting to creep me out.

—*Shirley*, FRANKLIN, MA

This can't be good, Shirley,

Vultures at your back door? Have you taken attendance lately? Is there a family member you haven't seen in a while? I like birds, but this would creep me out, too. Of course, I believe you. Why would you make this up? Having vultures pecking at your house is not something most people brag about, unless they live in Death Valley.

Turkey Vultures are large, dark birds with a six-foot wingspan. (I know you know this, Shirl. This information is for the folks who aren't lucky enough to have their own vultures.) They are most often seen soaring high overhead, like hawks. Because of their size, many people think they are eagles. However, eagles tend to glide with their wings held flat. Turkey Vultures hold their wings in a shallow V-shape, like the cushion of a couch with a hefty guy sitting on it.

Although vultures eat meat and soar like hawks and eagles, we aren't sure if they are related to other birds of prey. Some of the eggheads believe they are more closely related to herons and storks. Storks? It's bad enough having a vulture on your deck, could you imagine if it was delivering your baby? Come to think of it, I think I've met a few of those kids.

Vultures don't kill stuff. Like most of us, they only eat animals that have been killed by something else. And unlike most other birds, vultures have an excellent sense of smell. They are able to locate food by sniffing out the wonderful aroma given off by rotting carrion. A vulture's sense of smell is so reliable that at one time gas companies would watch for vultures near their pipelines.

111

(Apparently, the odor in the gas is similar to the stink given off by carrion.) If they spotted a flock of vultures circling around a section of pipeline, there was a good probability the pipe had a leak. I know this sounds like a made-up story, but this vulture/pipeline thing is true. Really, I'm not that creative.

As for your problem, Shirley, I've learned this situation is more common than you might think. Down south, vulture attacks on houses are not rare at all. The experts theorize that some building materials give off a smell that the birds once again interpret as rotting carrion. What looks like a beautiful vinyl screen door to you, may smell like a scrumptious dead mule to a Turkey Vulture.

Stopping the birds is tricky because they are federally protected, so you can't be mean to them. Some garden shops sell motion detectors that squirt water when something gets too close. They are used to scare pests out of people's gardens. Something like that may spook your vultures and save your house from being eaten. In the meantime, do what I suggested earlier: take a head count. Maybe you have a dead relative lying out back. In that case, you won't have to buy that water squirter I just mentioned. Talk about a lucky break.

6.

Don't Forget Cities Have Birds, Too

Birds are amazingly adaptable creatures. If they can find food and shelter, they'll be there. Concrete and asphalt have driven many species of birds away from the inner city, but not all of them have left. A number of birds have developed a taste for tall buildings, rats, and scraps of old hot dogs; they find cities to be an oasis. Anyone living in a city shouldn't give up on birds. They make the concrete less gray. And besides, without birds, think how lonely the statues would be.

Big-City Lifestyle Suits Peregrine Falcons Just Fine

Dear Bird Folks,
This fall I was in Boston on a business trip. One morning, as I looked out the window of my hotel room, I saw a Peregrine Falcon sitting on the roof of the building next door. I'm including this photo as proof because the books tell us that Peregrine Falcons live on mountain cliffs. Yet here is one right in the middle of a major city. Isn't this a bit unusual?

—*James,* SPENCER, WV

You're a good-looking man, James,

Although I've never met you, I got an idea of what you look like from the photo you sent. While I can barely see the image of the bird, I can clearly see your reflection in the window. I can also see the reflection of a blonde lady standing behind you. Who's that, the chambermaid? Sure, let's go with that. I don't want to tell you what to do, but maybe you should edit the photo a bit before you have it framed and hung over your fireplace at home.

The story of the Peregrine Falcon is interesting (if you like this kind of stuff). Peregrines have long been considered to be the world's fastest bird. How fast? It's still a topic of debate but many experts believe they can dive at speeds exceeding 200 mph. Not debatable, however, is that they are one of the most widespread birds on earth. The word peregrine, in fact, means "wanderer." How's that for a piece of useless trivia?

These birds can be found from Canada to Argentina, from Europe to Africa, from Asia to Australia. In the Americas, peregrines are known to make extremely long annual migrations. Birds that nest in the northern tundra often spend the winter in Argentina, a round trip of over fifteen thousand miles. Unfortunately for the birds, those extra frequent flyer miles do them little good since the best migration days are always blacked out.

Peregrines have been used for centuries in the unsettling blood sport of falconry. One bird is trained to kill another bird for entertainment. Peregrines are always pictured sitting on a big leather glove, wearing those ridiculous-looking hoods on their heads. Falconers say the hood helps keep the birds calm, but I think the birds are so embarrassed by the whole event that they wear it to hide their identity.

Although never truly endangered, certain populations of Peregrine Falcons suffered dramatic losses during the mid-1900s. Most of us probably remember the disastrous consequences from the use of DDT. While DDT didn't have any deadly effects on adult birds, it caused the females to lay eggs with thinner shells, which often broke before hatching. Without young chicks to take the place of the aging adults, Peregrine Falcons began disappearing, particularly in eastern North America. With the banning of DDT, along with reintroduction programs from organizations such as the Peregrine Fund, the falcon population has been recovering.

Historically, Peregrine Falcons are birds of wide-open spaces, mountain cliffs, and wild coastlines, where they prey on ducks and shorebirds. To see one of these speedy birds, you had to get away from civilization. Over the past few decades, however, more falcons are finding the urban landscape to their liking. Clock towers, tall bridges, and building ledges have replaced mountain cliffs; pigeons and starlings are substituting for ducks and shorebirds.

In some cities falcons have become so popular that many municipalities have set up webcams. By simply switching on your computer, you can watch falcons nesting on top of the local high-rise. It used to take a lot of traveling and a little luck to see one of these birds in action. Now you can watch them all day without having to get out of your PJs. That's my kind of bird watching.

I'm surprised you haven't heard about peregrines in cities, James. It seems every spring some newspaper or television station has an urban falcon story. Here's mine. I was walking down Constitution Avenue in Washington, DC, when I spotted a Peregrine Falcon high overhead. The bird eventually landed on the massive IRS building. As I watched, I couldn't help feeling that something wasn't right. It's not that falcons shouldn't be in the city; we've already established that this has become commonplace. What struck me as odd is that the falcon chose the Internal Revenue Service building to perch. I mean, if any bird is going to feel comfortable on the IRS headquarters, shouldn't it be a vulture?

Birding in Central Park

Dear Bird Folks,
I'm going to New York City on business and may have time to do some bird watching. I've heard that Central Park offers decent birding. Do you know if this is true and if it would be worth my while to take my binoculars with me?
—Chad, HARRISBURG, PA

Of course, Chad,
You should always take your binoculars anytime you travel, but especially to NYC. Over the years I've saved thousands of dollars on theater tickets. I purchase the cheapest seats and use my binoculars to make it seem like I'm in the front row. I can see everything

perfectly, even the spit flying out of the actors' mouths, yet I stayed nice and dry in the cheap seats. One time I even took my spotting scope to a show and it worked great . . . except for the guy in front of me complaining that my scope kept hitting him in the head. What a crybaby. He was mad that he didn't think of it first.

Your timing couldn't have been better. I just returned from New York City and actually did some birding. It was my first visit there in years. I've refused to go until Broadway stopped showing that despicable musical, *Cats*. (An entire show about cats? Can you imagine anything more disgusting?)

Like you, I heard that Central Park offered good birding, but I didn't really believe it. Who wants to deal with an old, rundown city park to see a handful of House Sparrows and starlings, or pigeons with graffiti spray-painted on them? I could not have been more wrong. The day I was there, the park was stunningly beautiful. Spring flowers were coming up, trees were blossoming, and the fountains were all going. Plus, the park is free and open to everyone. Free! In New York! Can you imagine?

A customer told me the best place to find birds in Central Park is an area called "the Ramble," so that's where I headed. (Remember, it's the "Ramble," not the "Bramble," as one idiot kept saying. Okay, the idiot was me, but let's move on.) The Ramble is a thirty-eight-acre section of the park that is wooded, quiet, and secluded. There are plenty of well-marked trails, benches creatively made from twisted logs, and even a stream. I kept expecting to meet a family of Hobbits. There were no Hobbits, but I did find plenty of birds. In this small area, only few hundred yards away from the cabs, crowds, and gridlock, I saw assorted woodpeckers, thrushes, swallows, egrets, kinglets, and warblers. Birds were everywhere.

Unfortunately, I wasn't able to spend much time in the park. It was my wife's birthday, and I had just given her a $5 gift card to Tiffany's on Fifth Avenue and she was itching to use it, or at least part of it. Still, in only an hour of birding in the Ramble I saw over thirty species of birds. If I've done the math right, that works out to a new bird every two minutes. That's not bad, especially in mid-April, especially in the middle of a huge city, and especially for me. The Ramble, and the area around it, boasts a life list of 230 birds and is often cited as one of the top birding spots in the country. Who knew?

It's easy to see why birds would stop off at Central Park. For miles around there's nothing but brick and cement and New Jersey, so landing in the park is the best option. How the birds manage to weave their way through skyscrapers, massive bridges, and blinding lights is mind-boggling, but they somehow do it. (They are probably guided by the smell of fresh bagels.)

The Ramble is located in the middle of the park, somewhere around 74th Street. If you go, walk over to the small pond where kids operate miniature remote-controlled sailboats. On the west side of the pond, you'll find a group of dedicated folks watching the nest of the park's legendary Red-tailed Hawk, Pale Male. For a small donation, they'll let you watch Pale Male through one of their powerful scopes. If you do, Chad, put in a buck for me. I owe them a donation. I blew all my money on that $5 gift card to Tiffany's.

The Legend of Pale Male

Dear Bird Folks,
This is not a question but rather a suggestion for you and your readers. I saw a showing of The Legend of Pale Male *at a local film festival. I really enjoyed it and think you might, too. Although Cape Cod probably doesn't have a film festival, you may be able to find this movie playing in Boston or Cambridge. It's well worth seeking out.*

—Brandon, GEORGETOWN, WASHINGTON, DC

Wait one minute, Brandon,

What do you mean, "Cape Cod probably doesn't have a film festival"? This isn't Black Fly, Newfoundland. Cape Cod has at least three film festivals, and some of them even show "talkies." The Provincetown Film Festival, for example, is a wonderful event for seeing new and unusual movies. Where else can you see a biopic about a mutant sand dune or a documentary about the invention of clam chowder, with subtitles, while eating Portuguese fried dough?

In addition to the fabulous movies, there is no shortage of celebrities to be seen at this festival. One year John Waters and Kathleen Turner had lunch at a table right next to mine. Unfortunately, some idiot kept winking and blowing kisses to Ms. Turner while she was trying to eat. He created such a scene the restaurant owner had to come over and ask me to leave.

I attended this year's Provincetown Film Festival and actually saw the film you suggested . . . although I have to admit it wasn't my first choice. I went to the festival with my friend Olivia. In addition to being a good friend, she also edited this book. Check the opening page if you don't believe me.

As a reward for her hard work, I let her choose the movie. She chose *The Legend of Pale Male*. I was not happy. Not only did I have my heart set on seeing the chowder film, but I hate those sappy, anthropomorphic bird movies. I didn't want to spend two hours watching a majestic bird of prey turned into a sentimental, romanticized figure. As usual, I was wrong. The movie is awesome, a thousand times better than I thought it would be.

For anyone who doesn't already know, Pale Male is the name of a Red-tailed Hawk, the first red-tail to nest in NYC in nearly a century. This bird wasn't about to build its nest in an isolated tree; he chose the ledge of an exclusive high-rise overlooking Central Park. Throughout the movie, we were treated to lots of amazing footage of this powerful raptor; but the movie has little to do with hawks or, for that matter, any other birds. It's about nature, human nature. As the story unfolds, we meet an endless stream of characters who regularly came to watch this hawk. It sounds lame, but it's not.

Pale Male's nest is under constant surveillance by hawk watchers, plus a conglomeration of local freaks and weirdoes. Pale Male's fans are the kind of people most of us would cross the street to avoid. But as the movie continues, they slowly become less weird and far more charming. Eventually, instead of wanting to avoid them, I wanted to join them. They were dedicated, caring, and completely supportive of each other. Almost none of them knew each other before Pale Male came to town, but they met at the same bench—day in and day out, year in and year out, rain or shine—to monitor the activity around the bird's nest.

A movie can't be a movie without a bit of ugliness, and that ugliness was provided by the boneheads who lived in the exclusive high-rise. After letting Pale Male and his assorted mates raise their chicks on the same ledge for ten years, the landlords, without warning, ripped the nest down. They claimed they were tired of all the attention their building was getting. As you can imagine, the plan backfired. Their building received way more attention than ever before, which forced the boneheads to grudgingly reverse their decision. The nest was replaced, the hawks returned, and everyone cheered, even me. (Don't tell anyone.)

Thanks for the recommendation, Brandon. *The Legend of Pale Male* is totally not the sappy bird movie I feared it would be. It's a bird movie . . . about people. Bird watching—like golf, dog walking, and gardening—is something that gets us up in the morning. People who spend their day staring at a bird's nest may seem weird to some, but they are doing what is meaningful to them, and there's nothing wrong with that. At least none of them were blowing kisses at Kathleen Turner. Only a real weirdo does that.

City Turkey

Dear Bird Folks,
Perhaps you have heard of Cambridge's resident male Wild Tur-
key, known as Mr. Gobbles. He is extremely well fed, but lacks any
female companionship. At the appropriate time of year, he displays
the mating plumage, but I've never seen any activity on that score
(no pun intended). Isn't the mating imperative a stronger motiva-
tor than a constant feeding source?

—Margaret, MELROSE, MA

Nope, not me, Margaret,

I hate to say it, but living here in the wilds of the outer Cape, I don't have direct knowledge of the avifauna wandering the streets of Cambridge, Massachusetts. In other words, I have no idea who Mr. Gobbles is. But judging from his uppity name, he sounds more like a bird that should live across the Charles River on Beacon Hill. Are you sure this turkey isn't called Professor Gobbles? That has more of a Cambridge-y ring to it.

If the male turkey's breeding habits are anything like his male human counterparts', I'd say Mr. Gobbles' age could be a factor. When choosing between breeding and eating, young human males will choose eating every time. Boys find food far more satisfying and a lot less complicated. The same thing could be said for middle-aged men. Give them a good meal, Margaret, and they'll leave you alone, whether you like it or not.

However, the males that fall between these two age groups are always ready for action. They'd rather starve than pass up an opportunity at intimacy, or as you so warmly refer to it, "the mating imperative." What we need is to find out how old the Gobster is. Don't stress about it because I've done the research for you. The birth records I found in the Cambridge City Hall are a

bit sketchy, but it seems that your Mr. Gobbles (if that is his real name) is at least four years old. With an average life expectancy of two years, four is old for a turkey. In human years, Mr. Gobbles is pushing 156.

At this advanced age, mating becomes less important than his daily nap. After lunch, it is most likely that old man Gobbles would rather look for a warm spot in which to nod off than spend the day trying to track down a female. The mating imperative has passed him by.

Age aside, the major reason Mr. Gobbles isn't getting any action is the 'hood. He could strut around all day gobbling his head off and still not attract a mate because there's none to attract. Cambridge isn't exactly a hotbed of available female turkeys. Unless your turkey has access to some kind of Internet dating service, he could remain a bachelor for a long time.

Before you start feeling bad for the G-man, keep in mind that life in Cambridge is pretty good for him. He has direct access to museums, tons of great coffee shops, and, if he ever wants to monitor a class at MIT, no one would notice him; he'd blend right in.

Finally, Margaret, let's not forget that Mr. Gobbles has lived twice as long as the average turkey. Perhaps there are more important things in life than mating. I never thought those words would come from me, but it may be true. I'd write more but I've just finished lunch and it's time for my nap.

City Bird Assortment

Dear Bird Folks,
I live in a fairly urban environment just outside of Boston. We have a bird feeder the local sparrows love. Unfortunately, they are the only birds we get. If our yard can attract so many sparrows, why doesn't it attract other birds as well?

—Amy, SOMERVILLE, MA

Not Somerville, Amy,

No offense, but I had a wicked disappointing experience in Somerville. A few years ago I saw poster announcing "The Annual Somerville Honk! Festival." The Honk! Festival? While the poster didn't explain what the Honk! Festival was, I assumed it was a festival held to honor Canada Geese. It's about time a community had an event to show appreciation for these much-maligned birds. I had to go.

On the day of the festival I arrived early, wearing my "I Love a Good Goose" T-shirt. That's when I found out it had nothing to do with birds. It seems the Honk! Festival is about street musicians. "Honk" refers to people playing horns and other instruments.

Whoever heard of a festival being about music and not geese? It was one of the biggest disappointments of my life . . . and I'm a Red Sox fan, so I know about disappointment.

In many cities, the three most common birds are Rock Pigeons (aka, pigeons), European Starlings, and your friends, House Sparrows. These three birds have one thing in common: they are all non-native, just like most of us. These foreign birds were brought to this continent because some Europeans wanted the New World to be like the Old World. (The birds that were already here weren't good enough.) Many species of birds were introduced, but most of them couldn't hack it and failed to generate a sustainable population. But pigeons, starlings, and sparrows are amazingly adaptable birds and they thrived.

Historically, Rock Pigeons nested on cliffs and rock ledges (hence their name). Over the centuries pigeons have slowly substituted building ledges and bridge girders for rock ledges. Sparrows and starlings, on the other hand, like to build their nests in holes. It doesn't make any difference to them if the holes are in a tree trunk or a CVS sign. Since there are thousands of artificial nesting holes in every city, these birds found it easier to live in town rather than commute from suburbia.

In addition to having an abundance of nesting locations, cities offer an array of food choices. When the House Sparrows arrived here in the mid-1800s, our streets were literally paved with food. Back then horses were the primary source of transportation. The sparrows readily gobbled up leftover grain spilled by the sloppy horses. The birds were also clever enough to pick out undigested seeds from the ever-present horse manure. (You know a bird is adaptable when it doesn't mind searching for food in a steaming pile of manure.) When automobiles replaced horses, the birds quickly shifted gears and started consuming food dropped by a species even sloppier than horses . . . humans.

Right now you must be thinking, "If cities are so bountiful, why don't the native birds take advantage of them, too?" Adapting to environmental changes takes time. Pigeons, starlings, and sparrows had already learned how to deal with European cities long before they came here. They arrived pre-adapted (if there is such a word). The destruction of habitat and craziness of civilization were too much for the native birds. Most of them took the trolley to the end of the line and kept going.

This is not to say a few cardinals, chickadees, finches, etc., aren't seen in cities. They certainly are, but the lack of proper nesting sites and natural food sources makes it tough for native birds to flourish. Plus, they have trouble competing with the more aggressive city birds. (You know how pushy those city types can be.)

In addition to being more aggressive and adaptable, city birds have something else going for them. They may actually be smarter. (I know that's a word.) A recent study found that city birds, with their ability to avoid canyons of glass buildings, herds of rushing pedestrians, and packs of rabid taxis, actually have larger brains than their country cousins. I'm not too surprised, though. City birds should be smarter, since they are surrounded by the best colleges, universities, and museums. Pigeons love art so much they make regular "contributions" to every statue they find.

While pigeons, starlings, and sparrows are the current urban avian kings, it doesn't mean it will stay that way. As I said earlier, adapting to environmental changes takes time. We've already seen falcons and hawks nesting on urban high-rises. I wouldn't be surprised if more native species followed their lead.

Speaking of surprises, I plan to return to Somerville for this year's Honk! Festival. Maybe I'll see you there, Amy. Just keep in mind I'll be wearing my "I Love a Good Goose" T-shirt again, so please don't wear yours, too. That would be awkward.

7.

Being Free as a Bird Isn't Always That Great

There's something romantic about watching an eagle or even a gull soaring high overhead. Effortlessly gliding on a warm breeze sounds wonderful, but even a warm breeze has its dangers. Flying birds still have to dodge storms, power lines, and Sully Sullenberger's Airbus A320. The environment, either man-made or natural, can be tough on birds. Yet, through it all, most of them manage to figure it out . . . except those Canada Geese that encountered Sully's Airbus.

Birds and Power Lines—Sometimes It Works, Sometimes Not So Much

Dear Bird Folks,

Today I discovered a dead Blue Jay on my front lawn. The bird was in pretty good shape, except for being dead. As I stood there considering a possible cause of death, I looked up at the power lines running to my house. Do you think this Blue Jay could have landed on one of the wires and electrocuted itself?

—Diane, BREWSTER, MA

I'll get to your question in a minute, Diane,

Your note reminded me of something I saw on my way to work. I drove past a local seafood joint and noticed they had installed bug zappers near their outdoor eating area. Are they the only people in the world who haven't heard that bug zappers do more harm than good? Zappers incinerate thousands of beneficial insects while rarely killing mosquitoes or other nuisance insects. Some studies indicate they could actually spread disease. When the bugs hit the zapper they explode, spreading tiny insect parts around the area. Yum! I won't name which restaurant installed the lame bug zapper. This seafood restaurant is popular, with powerful owners. I don't want to wake up to find the head of a fried clam at the foot of my bed.

I know I started a bit off topic, Diane, but that zapper rant actually has something to do with your question. You mentioned the Blue Jay was in "pretty good shape, except for being dead" (cute line, BTW). I'm no Inspector Clouseau, but I doubt the jay had a problem with the power lines. If it had, the poor bird would have looked like a smoldering bug-zapper insect. But you are right to be concerned; power lines can be a problem.

In many ways birds benefit from power lines. Both the wires and poles are important resting locations for many birds, especially in areas with few trees. We've all seen hawks sitting on top of utility poles waiting for some furry creature to wander out in the open. Ospreys love those big poles to build their nests on. Each fall swallows gather by the hundreds on the power lines before starting their trip south.

I once thought birds didn't get fried because the wires are insulated, the way power cords to our electric appliances are insulated. Once again I was wrong. Only the power lines around homes are insulated; big transmission wires aren't protected by insulation at all. If you reached up and touched one, you'd be toast. Birds can safely sit on the bare wires because they aren't grounded. If I understand it right, I could jump up, grab a power line, and be fine . . . as long as I didn't touch the ground, a pole, a tree branch, or another wire. If I did, I would complete the circuit and become the fried special du jour.

Small birds, such as swallows and jays, may not have a problem with power lines, but many large birds do. Cranes, eagles, pelicans, and condors top the list of birds we continue to lose to power lines. When a large bird flies between wires and touches its wing tips to two different wires simultaneously, they complete the circuit and the result is bad.

It's not always electricity that causes a problem. Many birds are injured when they collide with transmission wires during bad weather. In some critical locations, pressure has been put on the power companies to either bury the lines, hang markers on them to make them more visible, or insulate them. Saving the birds can be in the companies' best interest. They may or may not care about birds, but they care if their equipment is damaged and service is interrupted. Even power companies don't like to listen to irate customers who are missing *American Idol* because the power went out.

Sorry about your jay, Diane. I wish I could tell you what happened, but I don't think your power lines had anything to do with it. It probably got ahold of a bad clam from that seafood joint up the street. But you didn't hear that from me.

Battling Hurricanes

Dear Bird Folks,
It's been days since Hurricane Irene blew through our area and I'm still sitting in the dark waiting for the electric company to restore my power. With so much time on my hands I've been wondering how the birds are doing. How do they deal with such powerful storms?
—Sheryl, MARION, MA

They're smart, Sheryl,

Birds are able survive storms because evolution has provided them with the instincts to deal with all sorts of environmental hazards. Birds also can learn. Through trial and error and by watching others of their species, birds quickly learn to avoid deadly pitfalls. Most creatures with higher intelligence have the ability to learn from their mistakes. The exception to this rule, of course, is electric company executives. No matter how many times their utility poles are knocked down by storms, they put them back up in the same spots. Evidently, all the dodos aren't extinct.

Hurricanes are complicated weather systems. Hurricane Irene sent plenty of wind to my house, but not a drop of rain. Meanwhile, the poor folks a few miles away got enough rain to make Noah nervous. Birds' responses to such storms are equally complicated. Seabirds, for example, tend to ride along with the powerful winds until they can safely escape. Sometimes they end up hundreds of miles from their normal range, where they are greeted by dozens of work-skipping birders.

Songbirds, on the other hand, drop into low foliage and ride out the storm by clinging to branches with their strong feet. But woodpeckers may be the smartest of the bunch. They avoid storms by hiding in tree cavities. That works until the tree gets knocked down. Then they are on the phone with their insurance company, just like the rest of us.

Shorebirds, living on exposed mudflats, seem to be the most vulnerable. But they have learned to drop behind the nearest dune or ridge to avoid the ravaging winds. Last fall I was birding from my car near a local beach. As I watched a flock of Dunlins (sandpipers), the sky suddenly became black and a fierce squall roared across the harbor. Storm clouds poured sheets of rain and hail, while gale-force winds sandblasted the paint off my car. Through all the craziness I kept my eyes on the Dunlins. The wind arrived so fast and with such fury a few birds were actually knocked over like bowling pins before they could react. They quickly recovered and took to the air.

I expected them to fly as fast as they could to get away from the pocket of nasty weather. However, they flew about twenty feet and dropped into a shallow depression behind some beach grass. They hunkered down and the fierce winds blew right over them. After the winds subsided, the birds went back to feeding as if nothing happened. I learned two things that day: first, shorebirds know how to deal with strong winds; second, next time I go to the beach when there are storms around I should borrow someone else's car.

It has long been theorized that birds can predict approaching storms. This was clearly evident with Irene. Almost all my customers reported seeing more birds than usual on their feeders the day before the storm. Even during the height of the storm, many people saw birds on their feeders, which were nearly horizontal in the wind. The most logical reason for this extra food consumption is to provide the birds the energy needed to deal with the nasty weather. There's also another little-known theory that has to do with weight gain. The birds think that the fatter they are, the less likely they'll be blown away. I totally subscribe to this theory. That's why I ate all the ice cream in our freezer . . . even before the power went out.

Most backyard birds are ultimately affected very little by tropical storms, but it's a different story for migrating birds, many of which fly over the open ocean. When they run into bad weather, they do their best to fly over or around it, but sometimes they can't. When this happens the birds eventually become exhausted and end up in the oceanic food chain.

But this is not always the case. It seems one particular bird, which was being tracked by researchers, did just fine. A Whimbrel (another sandpiper) named "Chinquapin" left its breeding grounds in Canada and headed out over the Atlantic, only to run into Irene. It somehow battled the hurricane for four days without landing. Finally, the tired bird managed to set down on a beach in the Bahamas, where it was immediately approached by a local who tried to sell it a shell necklace and a timeshare.

Birds have been dealing with hurricanes for centuries, Sheryl, and for the most part their instincts and ability to learn have served them well. It's too bad the big shots at the electric companies can't figure out that hanging power lines on exposed poles isn't the best way to keep them out of harm's way. I guess things could be worse. The wastewater department could hang sewer lines from poles. And we thought bird poop dropping from the sky was gross.

Birds Care about Which Coffee You Drink

Dear Bird Folks,
While shopping on Beacon Hill, I noticed one of the fancy shops selling shade-grown coffee, which is supposed to be "bird friendly." Does shade-grown coffee actually benefit birds or is it another way for fancy shops to charge fancy prices by adding a fancy name?
—*Bill,* BOSTON, MA

Wow, Bill,
You sure have a fancy vocabulary. Beacon Hill must be rubbing off on you. I really like going to Beacon Hill, too, but I was kicked out of there once for walking my dog. My dog wasn't wearing a

sweater, and that's unacceptable in that part of town. (I'm lucky I wasn't arrested.) But I shouldn't make fun of the Beacon Hill crowd. A local socialite, Harriet Hemmenway, who lived just a few blocks from the Hill, started the Audubon Society. Sure, she was fancy, but her efforts did more to help critters than anyone up to that point in history, except maybe Noah.

I understand why you might be suspicious about a product based on a gimmicky name. It wasn't long ago when many of us gobbled up gallons of Häagen-Dazs, thinking it was some kind of sophisticated Copenhagen-ish dessert, only to discover we were eating ice cream made by two guys in the Bronx. Häagen-Dazs was an exotic-sounding name they dreamed up to help sell their product. I can't blame the Bronx boys, though. Their original name, "Cousin Frankie's Frozen Stiffs," didn't have the right ring to it.

Then there was the "mountain grown" coffee ad campaign. Remember that? We were led to believe one company's coffee was special because it was mountain grown. It turns out that most coffee is grown in the mountains. Once again, the name or description meant very little. However, this is not the case with shade-grown coffee. Growing coffee in the shade is important. Before I explain, here's a little coffee history for you. (You may want to grab a large cup of joe right now to help you stay awake.)

It is believed the people living in the highlands of what is now Ethiopia were the first to use coffee. However, these people ate the beans and never made "coffee" from them. Who needs a hot drink in Africa? The first use of coffee as a beverage can be traced to the mountains of the Arabian Peninsula, where it was commercialized by an ancient tribe of capitalists known as the "Starbuckians." From there, the coffee crop slowly spread throughout most of the world's tropical regions, eventually finding its way to the Americas.

For centuries coffee was grown under the canopy because coffee plants are sun sensitive. This practice also allowed the beans to mature slowly, resulting in more flavorful beans. This changed in the early 1970s, when a sun-tolerant coffee plant was introduced. While not as flavorful, it produced a higher yield, causing many farmers to cut down the canopy in favor of the new plants.

The higher yield came with a price, however. The new sun-tolerant coffee plants required more fertilizer, more pesticides, and more clear-cutting, which resulted in fewer birds. In the past thirty years almost half the coffee canopy cover has been lost to clear-cutting. That's not good. Many conservation organizations, including the Smithsonian, sounded the alarm.

Ninety percent of the birds that once lived in the area around coffee plantations disappeared in a matter of years. What many Americans don't realize is that birds lost to this method of growing coffee aren't just weird tropical birds most of us never knew existed in the first place. We are losing "our" birds, too. Orioles, catbirds, tanagers, hummingbirds, thrushes, and other birds that come to our yards each summer travel to the tropics to survive the winter. They also suffer when the coffee canopy is removed; they need the native trees for cover, feeding, and roosting.

Some people argue that shade-grown coffee costs more. Have you been to a coffee shop lately? In my town, hoboes stand on the corner asking, "Buddy, can you spare $4.75 for a cup of coffee?" A few cents more won't change a thing, except help keep our birds coming back each spring.

To answer your question, Bill, yes, yes, *yes*, shade-grown coffee does benefit birds. Not only should you buy it, you should seek it out. This is one of the easiest earth-friendly things you can do. You don't have to march in protest, chain yourself to a tree, or wear a tie-dyed shirt. Although you could wear a tie-dyed shirt if you want to; just don't wear it on Beacon Hill or you'll be banished from there like me and my sweaterless dog.

Pesticides Aren't as Healthy as They Sound

Dear Bird Folks,
The trees in my yard are full of new leaves, especially the fruit trees.
Soon they'll be covered with little black worms that will destroy
their yields. Usually I spray them with pesticides, but I've become
concerned about the birds that eat at the feeders next to the trees. Is
it safe to spray? I don't want to lose my fruit.

—*Tod,* PEMBROKE, MA

I'm with you, Tod,

Even though I'm a vegetarian, I'd rather eat fruit. I'd become
a fruitarian, but that name sounds wimpier than vegetarian. Fruit
has it all over vegetables. Most fruits are sweeter than vegetables,
you don't have to cook them, and they make better desserts than
vegetables. There is apple pie, blueberry cobbler, raspberry turn-
overs, banana bread, and strawberry shortcake, to name a few.
What desserts do vegetables give us? Carrot cake? Oh, please.

Whether you like fruit, vegetables, or both, we aren't the only
ones who like them. That's where the problems come in. Since
humans first decided that growing food was better than chasing
after it with clubs, we have been fighting off the hordes of other
creatures that mistakenly thought we like to share. Over the years,
everything from fire to prayer to voodoo to chemicals has been
used to protect crops; all (but prayer and voodoo) have had environmental impacts. The first-known chemical insecticides, made
from sulfur, were used by the Sumerians forty-five hundred years
ago. I'm not sure who the Sumerians were, but if they used sulfur
they probably came from northeastern New Jersey.

Over a billion pounds of toxic pesticides are dumped on this
country each year; most of it doesn't come from commercial farmers but from homeowners. People like you and me, Tod, are do-

ing more than our fair share of spreading these poisons around. The patch of green emptiness we call a lawn is a major target, but ornamental shrubs and, yes, prized fruit trees are also sprayed, dusted, and powdered with nasty stuff.

The benefits are immediate. We get a greener lawn, redder roses, and spotless fruit. The long-term effects aren't as obvious. How these sprays affect the people who eat the fruit or the children who play on the lawn isn't as clear. What is clear is pesticides are bird killers. Birds are a hundred times more sensitive to pesticides than mammals. It is estimated that in the United States over sixty million birds die annually from pesticide exposure. We don't find that many bird bodies on the ground because they are quickly scooped up by scavengers or fast-food restaurants. Also, pesticides indirectly cause bird mortality: insect-eating birds and their nestlings may starve if spraying eliminates the insects in an area.

Birds' mobility is part of the problem. Because they fly, it's nearly impossible to keep them away from a recently treated area. Birds die from direct contact with pesticides or from eating the insects or plants that have been sprayed. They die from absorbing toxins when they land on a treated tree or plant. They die after drinking water contaminated by runoff. It doesn't have to be runoff either. Hummingbirds often obtain moisture by sipping water droplets that form on the leaves of a tree. If those leaves have been sprayed, the tiny birds are in big trouble.

Based on the above information, Tod, you can probably guess that I'm giving a giant thumbs-down to your question about spraying to protect your fruit trees. An easy alternative to spraying is to encourage more birds to your yard. Birds would love to feed those "little black worms" to their nestlings, especially if the worms aren't dusted with poison. In addition to your feeders, putting out a birdbath, setting up more nest boxes, and encouraging the growth of native vegetation will draw even more worm-eating birds to your yard.

For the sake of the birds, and perhaps even yourself, avoid using pesticides. Like that Joni Mitchell song says: "Give me spots on my apples but leave me the birds and the bees." Good luck with your fruit trees, Tod. Before I end I'd like to make a deal with you. I won't tell any bird watchers you once used pesticides if you don't tell anyone I've been listening to Joni Mitchell. Deal?

The Disappearing Song of the Wood Thrush

Dear Bird Folks,
When I was a kid I used to hear the beautiful song of the Wood Thrush in the woods near my house. Now I don't hear it anymore. Has something happened to them or have my ears gotten so bad that I can't hear birdsongs anymore?

—*Floyd,* GREENFIELD, MA

Probably both, Floyd,

Part of the problem could be your ears. As we get older it becomes more difficult for some of us to hear higher frequencies, especially those found in many birdsongs. I'm not saying you're old, but your name suggests you aren't a teenager. Kids are at my house every day and I've never heard one of them say that Floyd is coming over to play video games. However, when I go to the post office, there's always a pod of retired men yapping out front and at least half of them are Floyds.

If I could play the song of the Wood Thrush so that everyone reading this could hear it, I bet most people would say, "Hey, I've heard that song before." Like the smell of balsam reminds folks of Maine, Christmas, or cheap air fresheners, the unforgettable song of the Wood Thrush brings back memories of walking in the woods on a summer's evening.

Wood Thrushes are chubby, medium-sized songbirds. They are closely related to American Robins, and in poor light the two birds look similar. In better light it's easy to see that robins have slate-black backs and their signature brick-red breasts, while Wood Thrushes have rusty-brown backs and spotted fronts, looking like a sloppy house painter.

The Wood Thrush's habitat of choice is not our front lawns but deep, dark woodlands, where they spend most of their day on the ground searching for food. The forests in which these birds breed are often so dense the birds can't be seen, even by each other. As a result, these thrushes have developed a song that not only helps them attract a mate but is one of the most haunting sounds in the bird world.

When I say the Wood Thrush's song is "haunting" I'm not exaggerating. Like most birds, thrushes have a syrinx (voice box). The syrinx contains two membranes that vibrate when the birds sing. However, unlike most birds, the Wood Thrush is somehow able to separately control the vibration of each membrane, producing two distinct sounds simultaneously. The bird essentially sings a duet with itself, which explains its colloquial name, "the Sonny and Cher Thrush." Actually, that's a name I made up, so you probably won't find it in many bird books . . . yet.

The population of this musical wonder has been declining over the past few decades. In some locations the number of breeding thrushes has dropped by nearly forty percent. As you may have guessed, habitat change is a big part of the problem. Wood Thrushes spend the colder months in Mexico and Central America, where clear-cutting has negatively altered their wintering grounds. Thrushes typically return to the same forests each winter. If the forests have become, say, orange groves, the birds must find a new place to live. Many of the displaced birds will spend the winter wandering the tropics and eventually fall victim to predation, never to fly north again.

The birds that do return to North America must deal with changes we've made to their breeding grounds. Many of their secluded forests have become a patchwork of roads, homes and wood lots. Wood Thrushes are fairly tolerant of humans, but that tolerance comes with a price. The closer the birds nest to humans, the more likely they will become victims of other creatures that also tolerate humans.

High on the predator list are raccoons and housecats; but the number one troublemaker is the Brown-headed Cowbird. Cowbirds don't eat thrushes; they lay their eggs in their nests. The adult thrushes somehow don't notice that they laid three beautiful blue eggs and one ugly brown one. They hatch all the eggs, then feed and raise whatever comes out of them, often to the detriment of the little thrushes.

Whatever shape your ears are in, Floyd, it is becoming more difficult to hear the duet-sounding song of the Wood Thrush. But don't stop trying. Their amazing song is worth going out of your way to hear. In fact, folks in the District of Columbia enjoy the Wood Thrush so much they made it their "state" bird. The lawmakers in Washington have chosen to honor a bird that can talk out of both sides of its mouth at once. Perfect.

We'll See Your Sparrow and Raise You a Squirrel

Dear Bird Folks,

As I prepare for another year of trying to keep those nasty English Sparrows from evicting or killing my bluebirds, I wondered if any

*species from this side of the Atlantic has ever been brought to Eng-
land. If so, is it causing headaches there like the English Sparrow
is here?*

—*Diane,* COOPERSTOWN, NY

We've sent them a doozy, Diane,

One of our creatures has found its way to England, and the
Brits hate it. A British friend of mine gets so enraged when he
talks about this creature you can almost see color in his face. Before I continue, I need to go on record and state that introducing
any species into a new ecosystem is a bad idea. While it may seem
like I enjoy telling this story, I'm not. I only enjoy the irony.

Can you guess the creature in question? Here are a few hints.
It is native to the Eastern half of North America. It's not a bird,
but it's associated with birds. Everyone reading this has seen this
creature before, and 99 percent of you have cursed about it at
least once in your life (some of you perhaps daily or even hourly).
If we were going to send one creature to England to pay them
back for sending us the House (English) Sparrow, this is the perfect choice.

The creature in question is *Sciurus carolinenis,* aka, the Eastern
Gray Squirrel. The gray squirrel has found its way to England and
is driving them nuts. To which I say: Welcome to our world.

No one is sure how our squirrels ended up in England, but most people believe they arrived in the 1800s. Some think they were brought over as pets or perhaps for an exhibit in the London Zoo. Can you imagine paying money to see a squirrel? As you may have guessed, it didn't take long for squirrels to spread throughout the country. This was bad news for Britain's resident squirrel, the European Red Squirrel. The red squirrel is England's only native squirrel, and the Brits love it. I never thought I'd write the words "squirrel" and "love" in the same sentence, but it's true. It seems the author Beatrix Potter wrote a story about a red squirrel, and ever since, everyone there gets all mushy at the sight of one, just like everyone here gets all mushy at the sight of a photo of skinny Elvis.

Obviously, it's an environmental tragedy when an introduced species displaces a native species, but I don't get the mushy part. The European Red Squirrel isn't the cutest thing I've ever seen. It looks like the American Red Squirrel except it has these crazy, unnerving ear tufts, which make it look like a cross between Don King and something out of a Steven King novel. Gray squirrels are larger, more aggressive, and a lot more daring than the little reds. They're also smarter. (That's not a slam against red squirrels; gray squirrels are easily the smartest creatures to ever walk the earth.) The grays will quickly consume any available natural food, and they'll dominate any and all bird feeders. Surprise!

What are the British doing to combat the advancing gray squirrel herds? Sometimes people try to drink their problems away, but in this case the Brits are trying to eat their problem away. Restaurants and pubs all over the country are promoting gray squirrel dishes (really). Squirrel pie and squirrel kabobs have found their way onto local menus, while butcher shops have fresh squirrels hanging in the window. Apparently, squirrel is considered a delicacy. It wasn't too many years ago (about 250 or so) when the British made fun of us backward Americans for eating squirrel. Remember that irony I mentioned earlier?

Another irony in this squirrel-versus-squirrel dilemma is that I couldn't help but be a little offended when I read disparaging comments about "our" squirrel posted on British websites. I don't know why; I've said my share of nasty things about gray squirrels. I think it's a family thing. It's okay for me to make wisecracks about my family, but it's quite different when someone else does it. (I just compared my family to squirrels. I'd better stop this analogy.)

I don't know if the gray squirrel has caused as many problems in England as the House Sparrow has caused here, Diane, but both countries would be better off if neither species had ever left home. And as much as I don't like seeing House Sparrows here, they aren't the worst creatures the Brits have sent us. Have you ever seen a Yorkshire Terrier? What's up with those things?

Birds and Planes—and You Think YOU Have Trouble with the Airlines

Dear Bird Folks,
In light of the "Miracle on the Hudson," in which a commercial airliner was brought down by a flock of Canada Geese, I'd like to know how common bird-plane collisions are. Also, what is being done to prevent further accidents?

—*Rick,* SALISBURY, MD

Miracle is right, Rick,

I think the entire world was enthralled by that story. I get chills just thinking about it. However, after watching every news story about Flight 1549, I couldn't find a single report that provided information about the geese. Were they okay? Were they treated at an area Audubon sanctuary? Were their family, friends, and flock notified? Since none of the reporters mentioned the birds' condition, I assumed they all did fine. Yeah, let's go with that.

It's clear that birds and planes don't mix well. The number of annual collisions is reported to be around seven to eight thousand, but I'm not sure how accurate that is. The actual number may be higher because reporting bird strikes is voluntary. Some airlines may decide that it's easier to hose off the bird guts and skip the paperwork.

Whatever the real number of annual strikes, it appears to be rising. In the early 1970s bird strikes weren't as common as they are now. Why the increase? There are more people and more planes to carry them. The number of corporate jets alone has quadrupled in recent years. (Don't blame me. I only have one.) In addition, development has pushed the birds out of their preferred habitats and into less desirable locations (i.e., noisy airports).

While many species have been negatively impacted by man's population growth, certain other species, like gulls and geese, have adapted to changes we've made to the environment and have thrived. Not surprisingly, gulls and geese are the two biggest avian problems for planes. We know that because there is actually a lab set up to identify the birds. When a bird hits a plane, the bird's remains, called "snarge" (no, that's not a typo), are packed up and sent to the Smithsonian, where glove-wearing eggheads pick through the snarge and play Name That Bird. By knowing which birds cause the most problems, they are better able to advise airports on how to prevent further collisions and more snarge.

Early attempts at scaring birds away from airports were a bit like the tactics some of my customers use to keep squirrels off their feeders: they run outside, screaming like idiots. While the screaming tactic worked, it was rather tiring, so more sophisticated methods were developed. These days, airports fire air cannons, blast shotguns, or let psycho border collies run loose.

While these methods have worked, habitat management has the best results. Like us, birds are attracted to food, water, and shelter, so special grasses and other vegetation with little or no bird appeal are planted. Mammal populations are kept in check, and water is prevented from accumulating. If these techniques don't work, more sinister methods are employed. Bird food is laced with airline food, and the poor birds don't have a chance.

Because some strikes are inevitable, planes are designed with impacts in mind. Jet engines are tested for durability—wait 'til you read this—by having real birds fired into them from bird cannons (you read that right, bird cannons). The companies are quick to point out that they don't use live birds. (Oh, okay. Then I'm sure the birds are fine with it.) Windshields and other important areas are also reinforced to prevent bird damage. But even with extra protection, impacts can cause serious damage. I've seen photos of dented nose cones and smashed windshields. One bird hit a plane with such force it actually opened one of those little bags of peanuts.

Even though bird accidents are a serious concern, Rick, it should be noted that only one out of every ten thousand flights hits a bird, and most of those strikes cause little damage. Worldwide, about ten people die annually as a result of birds hitting planes. While that's a terrible thing, especially for those ten people, the odds of being on a plane that has a major bird strike are pretty slim . . . but not as slim as the odds of your luggage arriving the same time you do.

The Loss of the Carolina Parakeet

Dear Bird Folks,
I recently saw a display of colorful birds labeled "Carolina Para-
keets." I had never heard of them. The label also said these birds
are extinct. How sad. When did they live? Were they ever found in
my area? Why did they disappear?

—*Judy,* HAZLETON, PA

Come on, Judy,

I'm not one to gripe about a bird question, especially one that doesn't include a complaint about squirrels, but your timing could be better. With only a few weeks until Christmas, the last thing I want to write about is extinction. Talk about a downer. Wouldn't you rather ask about French hens, turtledoves, or some other bird that's a little more Christmassy? Okay, fine. Extinction it is. Let me get some eggnog. That will help me get through it.

You're not alone, Judy. I bet few people in Hazleton, or any other town (including towns in Carolina), know much about the Carolina Parakeet. For such a distinctive bird, it really hasn't gotten much press. When it comes to extinct birds, most attention has been given to the shocking extermination of the Passenger Pigeon, a bird with a population that was once in the billions. Although the Carolina Parakeet may not have numbered in the billions, it was an abundant bird. But being abundant wasn't enough to save it from our missteps.

The Carolina Parakeet was the only native parrot in the continental United States. Like many parrots, it was strikingly colorful, with a bright green body and an even brighter yellow head and red face. Carolina Parakeets were parrots in every sense of the word, but you didn't have to travel to the steamy tropics to see them. They flew wild and free from the Great Lakes to the Gulf Coast, from the Atlantic Ocean to the Rocky Mountains. This par-

144

rot lived and bred in the same forests many of us walk in today. It also did little or no migrating, which meant it was tough enough to deal with North America's notoriously nasty winters. And that's before global warming had a chance to take the edge off.

So what happened? Well, farmers weren't big fans because the Carolina Parakeets liked to sample their crops. In fact, many farmers had bumper stickers on their horse-drawn wagons that read, "Carolina Parakeets: Taste Like Chicken." When the bumper stickers didn't work, the farmers turned to guns, our universal problem solver, and thousands of parrots were shot on sight. Hat manufacturers also blasted away at the birds because their colorful feathers looked swell atop rich women's heads.

In most situations, it would be hard to kill so many birds with bullets alone, but Carolina Parakeets had a quirky behavior that led to their rapid undoing. While most birds will totally flee at the sound of a gun, these parrots would return to the scene of the crime if some members of the flock weren't able to make a clean getaway. All a gunner had to do was hit a bird or two and the entire flock would return to "help" their wounded comrades. After that . . . well, you can guess what happened.

Guns weren't their only problem. These were birds of the forest and much of our nation's forests were cleared for agriculture, building material, and firewood. In addition, some researchers speculate that many parrots were also lost to diseases from domestic fowl. The birds also had a big problem from an unlikely source, honeybees. Carolina Parakeets needed natural tree cavities in which to build their nests; without cavities the birds couldn't successfully reproduce. The introduced honeybees also used tree cavities in which to build their hives. Often when the birds tried to enter a cavity, they were confronted by a swarm of angry bees. Suddenly, the farmers' guns didn't seem so bad.

Whatever the ultimate reason for the demise of the Carolina Parakeet, the last documented wild flock disappeared in 1904; the last captive bird, named "Inca," died in the Cincinnati Zoo in 1918. A creepy footnote to all this is that Inca passed away in the same flight cage in which "Martha," the last living Passenger Pigeon, had died a few years earlier. There was some bad karma with that cage.

The loss of the Carolina Parakeet is significant on many levels, Judy, not the least being that we lost our only parrot. How cool would it have been to look out on a snowy Christmas morning to see a flock of brilliantly colored parrots at our feeders? Few places in the world have a population of parrots that can handle cold weather, but we did . . . at least for a while.

8.

Birds Are Superstars—and Publishers and Hollywood Know It

When I was a kid, I sent away for a book entitled *The History of Hawks and Doves*. The book turned out to be a discussion between warmongers and peaceniks. It seems funny now, but not so much at the time. Since then, I have gotten better at choosing my bird-book titles, and the books have gotten better, too. Publishers and even Hollywood have realized that bird stories are popular. The list of sweet bird stories grows longer every day, and everyone from Hitchcock to Steve Martin has gotten into making bird movies. And believe it or not, the most widely read secret agent of the twentieth century was named after, of all people, a birder. Some things in life defy logic.

Bond, James Bond, Ornithologist

Dear Bird Folks,
I recently signed up for a Caribbean cruise. One of the items they suggested I bring is a book called Birds of the West Indies *by James Bond. I never knew James Bond wrote bird books. I thought*

he only wrote spy novels. Do you know about this book? Is it the same James Bond?

—Adam, ASHEVILLE, NC

Yes, no, and are you kidding me, Adam?

I don't mean to take an attitude with you, but sometimes it's hard to tell if someone is putting me on or simply hasn't thought the question through. Yes, I know about the book of which you speak. No, James Bond didn't write spy novels. James Bond is a fictional character in a series of spy novels written by Ian Fleming. Don't feel bad. I know people who buy Dr. Seuss books because they think Seuss was a doctor, when in fact he wasn't any kind of doctor. He was nothing but a compulsive rhymer. As far as I know they don't award doctorates for rhyming, except to Dr. Dre. (Ask your grandkids; they'll explain it to you.)

While James Bond, the secret agent, is fictional, there is a twist to this story. A very real ornithologist named James Bond did write *Birds of the West Indies*. It is this same James Bond who lent his name to the fictional British spy. Really. It's beyond ironic that the name of a geeky birder has become synonymous with style, sophistication, and the world's biggest babe magnet. I know what you're thinking. If Ian Fleming wanted to pick a birder who would denote elegance and class, why didn't he pick me? I've asked myself that question for years.

Here's the backstory. Ian Fleming was a British journalist who did a bit of spying on the side. During World War II, he worked with British Naval intelligence in an effort to keep the creepy Nazis from taking Gibraltar. The plan was called "Operation Goldeneye." Toward the end of the war, Fleming traveled to Jamaica for a naval conference and to check out the local rum. After a few days in Jamaica, he realized island life was way better than damp, gloomy old England. He eventually bought land in Jamaica, built a house, and dubbed his new residence "Goldeneye."

In 1952, while at Goldeneye, he started writing his first spy novel, *Casino Royale.* The trouble was, Fleming couldn't come up with a name for his main character. While he paced around Goldeneye trying to think of a name, a bird book on the table caught his attention. (Fleming was also a pretty serious bird watcher.) The book was *Birds of the West Indies*; the author's name was Bond, James Bond.

Back at the Academy of Natural Sciences in Philadelphia, the ornithologist who had written *Birds of the West Indies* was happily minding his own business, studying stuffed birds and eating Philly cheesesteaks. Birder Jim had no idea who Ian Fleming was or that his name was about to become famous.

When real-life James learned about fake-secret-agent James, it didn't impress him much; in fact, he found it amusing. After all, birder Jim was famous in his own right. He was one of the world's leading authorities on Caribbean birds and had won several awards for his ornithological work. Plus, the interest in 007 hadn't gone mainstream yet. That changed when it was revealed that John F. Kennedy, America's new president, loved the James Bond books. From then on, birder Jim started receiving fewer inquiries about birds and more calls asking about Miss Moneypenny. (Actually, one of those calls may have been from me.)

Eventually, the real Bond sent a friendly letter to Ian Fleming, who wrote back and admitted what he had done. Fleming didn't offer Bond any compensation other than unlimited use of the name Ian Fleming. He even said that if Bond discovered a new bird species, one that was "particularly horrible," he could name it an "Ian Fleming" as payback. (In case you are wondering, that never happened . . . probably because there is no such thing as a horrible bird.)

In 1966, in an effort to either cash in on the notoriety or set the record straight, Mary Bond, Jim's wife, wrote a book entitled *How 007 Got His Name.* It was a hit in Britain but unfortunately, was never made available in this country. I tried to get a copy to help me with this column, but the one copy I found cost $165! Forget that. (It's easier, and way cheaper, to simply make stuff up.)

Ian Fleming was a party boy, Adam, and his excessive lifestyle caught up with him in 1964, when he passed away at fifty-six. Ornithologist James Bond, living the boring birder life, made it to the respectable age of eighty-nine. Bond and Fleming didn't have much in common except that they liked birds. And you can bet that whenever either of them filled a bird feeder, the birdseed was always shaken, not stirred.

African Eagles Can't Compare to Ours

Dear Bird Folks,
I've done some behind-the-scenes work for several movies and TV shows. While I was working on one of the shows, an animal handler told me a little Hollywood secret. He said that if a scene required an eagle, they'd often use African Bald Eagles instead of American Bald Eagles because African eagles have much whiter heads. Is this true?

—*Scott,* LOS ANGELES, CA

Probably, Scott,

Hollywood has never liked the American Bald Eagle. In particular, they don't like the way our Bald Eagle sounds. Filmmakers hate to spend millions producing a dramatic outdoor scene only to have the scene spoiled when the star eagle lets loose with its little squeaky voice. It's embarrassing. The voice of our national symbol sounds like a cross between a dog toy and Betty Boop.

Voice coaches have tried to teach the eagles to speak from their diaphragms but it never works. To remedy this predicament,

Hollywood brings in Red-tailed Hawks to do voice-overs. Red-tails give those bone-chilling screams directors love. The problem is, red-tails are needy and temperamental, and often won't leave their trailer unless their endless demands are met. (Chocolate-covered squirrels and deep-fried chipmunks aren't as easy to find as you might think.) Now, according to you, Scott, our eagles are being replaced by foreign eagles. Even our birds are having their jobs outsourced.

Here's what I know about the African Bald Eagle: there isn't one. No such species with that name exists. The guy who told you that story was either telling you a tall tale or he was smoking something that should be used for medicinal purposes only. However, Africa does have a fish eagle, and it does have a white head. But the two eagles don't look enough alike to be used interchangeably. It should be obvious to most folks that they are two different birds. It would be like using me as a body double for Tom Cruise. It wouldn't work. I could get by as George Clooney maybe, but I'm much too tall to be a convincing Tom Cruise.

While the head of an African Fish Eagle is white, its white feathers also run down the front of its chest like a lobster bib. The African Fish Eagle is a large bird of prey and can be found just about anywhere in the southern half of Africa where there are fish. These powerful birds can capture and fly away with a fish weighing as much as four pounds. Sometimes they'll catch a fish that is too big for them to carry. But, like all fishermen, they don't like to give up a good catch. Instead of releasing the jumbo fish, an eagle will simply use its wings as oars and paddle the fish to shore. Then, after first having its picture taken with its catch, the bird is ready for lunch. While fish are their main food source, they are capable of taking larger prey, including flamingos, turtles, and small crocs. (I'm taking about reptiles, not those goofy shoe things.)

Even though fish eagles are excellent hunters, they aren't above stealing an easy meal. Occasionally, they'll swoop down and swipe a fish from unsuspecting herons and pelicans, which are quite helpless to do anything about it. After a good meal, fish eagles are basically done for the day. They spend much of their time sitting and watching the world go by. I have a sixteen year old who does the same thing.

As I mentioned earlier, the voice of the American Bald Eagle is kind of wimpy, but the African Fish Eagle's voice is nothing to be ashamed of. Their call is loud and haunting, sounding like a cross between a loon, a hyena, and England's Susan Boyle. The fish eagle's call is so distinctive that it is often referred to as "the voice of Africa." (The American Bald Eagle's sissy call is often referred to as "the voice of Munchkinland.")

I can't say for certain that Hollywood has never tried to pass an African Fish Eagle off as an American Bald Eagle, Scott. They can do amazing things with makeup. Look what they've done with Susan Boyle.

That Quail, Robert

Dear Bird Folks,

I just returned from Cape Cod. I stopped at your shop with a ques-tion, but neither of the two young saleswomen could answer it. I'd like to know where in Orleans Margaret Stanger, the author of That Quail, Robert, *lived. Many thanks.*

—John, UPSTATE NY

Sorry, John,

I'm sorry neither of my employees was able to answer your question, but as you said, they were "young." The story of *That Quail, Robert* happened over fifty years ago, a little before their time. You may have gotten a better response if you had asked them about books that were more current—like, perhaps, young vampire books. You are probably wondering why kids would rather read about hot-looking vampires instead of quail. I know, I don't get it either.

Margaret Stanger's book, *That Quail, Robert,* is without a doubt the most important twentieth-century literary work to come out of North America, or at least the Outer Cape. The regional signif-icance of her work can't be underestimated. Throughout history there have been icons who have drawn the world's attention to the location of their humble beginnings. Tupelo, Mississippi, has Elvis; Liverpool, England, has the Beatles. And Cape Cod, Mas-sachusetts, has a tiny quail named Robert. Some may argue that the Kennedys brought more attention to the Cape than Robert, but I don't see it. I mean, has anyone ever written a book about the Kennedys? If they have, I don't know about it, but I haven't been to the library in a while.

In case there is someone who has yet to read *That Quail, Rob-ert,* let me fill you in. Robert was born in the summer of 1962.

This was a time when Bobwhites were still regularly found on Cape Cod . . . before the cats, bulldozers, and trophy homes moved in. The adult quail built their nest on the edge of a yard that belonged to the Kienzle family. This pair of birds picked the right yard, because the Kienzles loved birds.

Like many ducks, quail are born ready to go. The entire brood, usually about fourteen eggs, hatches out and leaves the nest on the same day. That's just what Robert's siblings did—they hatched and headed off. The next day the Kienzles found the abandoned nest and an orphaned egg. They brought the egg into their kitchen, ran it under cold water, doused it with bug spray, washed it in dish detergent and left it on the counter as a decoration. Amazingly, three days after being deserted by his parents and washed with detergent, baby Robert chipped his way out of the "decoration." The little bird popped out of the egg healthy, happy, and quite content to be in a house filled with Kienzles.

For the next three years, Robert was a local and national star. Newspapers ran stories about this wild quail living the life of a family pet in Orleans. Thousands of people came from all over to see the charming quail that met guests at the door, led them to the sitting room, and softly chirped as he sat on their shoulders. In addition to his warm personality, he was housebroken and so self-confident he didn't mind being called Robert . . . even after he started laying eggs, which meant Robert was really Roberta.

Unfortunately, the Kienzles are no longer with us. Margaret Stanger, the Kienzle's friend, neighbor, quail babysitter, and author of *That Quail, Robert,* passed away in 1980. However, Cathy Baldwin, the book's illustrator, is very much alive, living in Orleans, and not one of the Baldwin brothers. Cathy was only a teenager when she first met Robert. She heard he was having a birthday party, so the young artist gave the family a watercolor of the little quail. Everyone liked Cathy's work so much she was asked to illustrate the new book about Robert's life. Could this story get any sweeter?

The house where Margaret Stanger lived and wrote, and where Robert stayed when his foster parents, the Kienzles, were away in Europe, is located at 47 Monument Road in Orleans. It's a private home, but there is a plaque on the road that tells of its avian and literary history.

Even though you can't go into Margaret Stanger's former house, John, you certainly can have your picture taken in front of it. Ms. Stanger's house is a regular Cape Cod house, built at a time when we had lots of quail, fewer cats, and typical Cape homes didn't have six stories and fifty-five rooms.

Turkeys Don't Come in Flocks

Dear Bird Folks,
While I was making my grocery list for Thanksgiving, I started wondering what a group of turkeys is called. We have a gaggle of geese and a covey of quail, but I've never heard a name for turkeys. It can't simply be a flock of turkeys, can it? That sounds too easy.
—Marie, ATHENS, GA

First—about that list, Marie,

I hope that grocery list of yours doesn't have "buy a turkey" on it. Just buy an extra squash or two and give the turkeys a break. If you won't do it for me, do it for Benjamin Franklin. Remember, old Ben wanted the Wild Turkey to be our national bird. (*Spoiler alert:* We get into this Ben/turkey thing more in the next chapter. If this is your dream topic, try to hang on until then.) I think it's totally un-American to serve our almost-national bird to your annoying relatives. Come on, Marie. Take a stand. Besides, if you serve your relatives squash or perhaps Tofurkey instead of real turkey, maybe they'll go somewhere else next year. It's worth a try.

A group of turkeys is called a "rafter." That piece of information came from a book by James Lipton, entitled *An Exaltation of Larks*. The reason I know of this book is because my birding buddy, Fahy, gave me a copy. Fahy loves language and finds terms for a collection of things fascinating. I think it's a lame excuse to write a book. And believe me, I know about lame reasons to write books.

A few terms make sense, but most of them, like a "murmuration of starlings," seem as if they were dreamed up by people who ate a batch of bad mushrooms. But as I read the book, I realized many of these terms seem silly to me because I'm unfamiliar with them. I would be shocked if someone walked in and told me he or she had just seen an "exaltation of larks." However, I didn't blink when you mentioned a "gaggle of geese." Gaggle is a far stranger word. (It reminds me of the face people make when I suggest Tofurkey at Thanksgiving.) The reason it doesn't seem odd is because I'm familiar with it.

Most people my age know a group of whales is called a "pod." We probably imagine a tight group of whales, like peas in a pod. Younger folks may be confused by the term. Instead of envisioning peas, they are likely to picture an iPod and have no idea what whales have to do with MP3 players. When I read that a group of turkeys is called a "rafter," it seemed silly to me. I pictured turkeys sitting along a beam in a barn. But after reading Lipton's book I learned that raft means a collection. If you take a collection of logs, tie them together, and float them on water, you have a raft. This language stuff is fun after all. Well, sort of fun.

A group of doves is known as a "dule." This also gave me the wrong image. I thought of a duel and imagined doves engaging in a gunfight with Aaron Burr. It turns out dule comes from the French word "deuil," meaning "mourning." A dove has a soft, mournful call (as if it had lost a duel with Aaron Burr). Teal, which are small ducks, are collectively known as a spring of teal. Want to guess why "spring" is used? If you are dopey like me, you imagined a nice spring day when the ice is off the ponds and the ducks have returned. That sounds like a perfect fit to me, but it's not even close.

Spring, in this case, has nothing to do with the season. The name comes from the fact that teal can take off from the water directly into the air. Many ducks must run along the water's surface in order to become airborne, but not teal. They spring into the air. (Could this be any more exciting?)

I think most people know that a group of crows is a "murder," but their cousins, the ravens, also have an unkind name, literally. They are called an "unkindness of ravens." Years ago, rumors were spread about adult ravens pushing their babies out of the nest before they can fly. The rumor is not true, and the Department of Social Services cleared all adult ravens of any wrongdoing, and yet the name continues.

A group of hawks is a "cast," because the birds cast off the falconer's arm. Herons are a "siege," because they patiently wait out

the fish. And the list goes on, Marie. There are nonbird terms in the book, too. A group of boys is a "rascal," a group of prisoners is a "pity." Finally, a group of relatives is known as an "annoyance." I'm not sure if an "annoyance of relatives" is an actual term, but if it isn't, it should be.

A Good Movie No One Saw

Dear Bird Folks,
I've seen ads for a movie that's supposed to be about bird watching.
The movie is called The Big Year. *Is it actually about bird watching? It doesn't sound very "birdie" to me.*

—Lance, ALBANY, NY

I don't blame you, Lance,

I saw those same ads and I was also unclear about the movie . . . and I'm in it. That's right. I'm in the movie. Well, some of my stuff is in it. Let me explain.

A while ago I got an e-mail from 20th Century Fox. They wanted to buy lots and lots of bird stuff (books, T-shirts, artwork, etc.). I was suspicious at first and almost deleted the e-mail. I had just sent $500 to help a Nigerian prince and never even received a thank-you card. But it turned out that 20th Century Fox really was making a movie about birding and they wanted to buy a lot of our merchandise to use as props!

The Big Year is a movie based on the book of the same name by Mark Obmascik. It's also a true story. In the birding world, when someone goes for a "big year," he or she will try to see as many different birds as possible over the course of 365 days. Each year, lots of birders try to do this. It's no different than bookworms trying to see how many books they can read in a year or caffeine freaks trying to see how many Starbucks they can visit. My wife has her own idea of a big year. She tries to see how many dresses she can buy, and each year she sets a new personal best.

Occasionally, birders take a big year to extremes. Instead of going birding whenever they have free time, they go even when they don't have free time. Some of them don't go to work or school or attend birthday parties. They become obsessed with trying to see more birds in a year than anyone ever has. They want to set a record. In 1998, the year the book covers, there wasn't just one crazy birder trying to set a record, there were three . . . and they were all trying to outdo each other.

What's odd about competitive birding is that there is no real prize. There's no cash reward or free Cadillac given to the winner. Birders willingly travel thousands of miles, max out their credit cards, and endure seasickness and clouds of biting insects merely to gain the admiration of people as wacky as they are.

Right now you might be thinking, "These people are idiots," and you wouldn't be far off. But competitive birders are no more idiotic than folks who risk their lives climbing Mt. Everest or spend months hiking the Appalachian Trail. Their only reward is a photo with a flag or a high-five from other smelly hikers. All these people might be a little crazy, but they could think the same thing about those of us who lie on the beach all summer or on the couch watching TV all winter. At least at the end of it they have a story to tell.

The other strange thing about a big year is there's no bird umpire overseeing everything. It's all on the honor system. With no real reward, there is no reason to lie. It's not like we are talking about a bunch of lazy, fried chicken–eating baseball players who are only in it for the money. Seeing birds is what these people live for, not fat contracts.

About the movie: Steve Martin, Owen Wilson, and Jack Black star in the film. Each one plays a birder who is trying to set the record for seeing the most birds in North America in a single year. Before the movie was released, it was obvious the stars weren't comfortable being in a "bird movie." During interviews, each actor seemed almost embarrassed about playing a bird watcher, like he had just done a commercial for diarrhea medicine.

As you can imagine, Lance, I saw the movie right away. It's not the crazy farce you might expect from the three stars. It's actually a sweet story about three guys with complicated lives, who are driven to do something many folks find odd. To the filmmaker's credit, the birders weren't stereotyped goofballs. Also, the scenery is gorgeous, which makes me feel bad for the people who spend the winter inside watching TV. Finally, a few of the props we sent actually made it onto the big screen, including a scene where Jack Black's character is reading my first book, *Why Don't Woodpeckers Get Headaches?* You probably heard me screaming in Albany.

All this birding talk makes me think I should go for my own big year. Maybe I'll start tomorrow. No, wait. Tomorrow is birdseed-delivery day. Perhaps the next day. Nope, I have to take my wife dress shopping. Man, I hate reality.

9.

A Bird Buffet

Book publishers like to have everything organized into chapters and then into topics and, if possible, even into subtopics. But sometimes people ask bird questions that resist being pigeonholed (wink). Writing a chapter solely dedicated to ducks getting cold feet or the birds contained in the *Twelve Days of Christmas* makes no sense, even by my nonsensical standards. Instead of writing a chapter about each of these topics, I blended them into one. Think of this section as the junk drawer in your kitchen: all the items in it don't seem to fit anywhere else . . . but they're all essential and can never be thrown away. It's the law.

And You Think YOUR Feet Are Cold

Dear Bird Folks,
As I watch ducks swimming in a nearby bay I wonder why their little thin feet don't freeze. After being out in the cold for only a short time, my toes are turning blue, yet the ducks glide past me with happy smiling faces. How can they stand such cold?

—*Julia,* ORLEANS, MA

Whoa, Julia,

Your line about ducks with "happy smiling faces" gives me a great idea. The Smiling Duck Café is the perfect name for a coffee shop. It would have duck pictures on the walls, duck coffee mugs, and anyone named Donald, Daffy, Huey, Dewey, or Louie gets free coffee. Soon Smiling Duck Cafés would be everywhere. Starbucks would have to change its name to "Starducks" to compete. I was just about to ask you to be my business partner when a quick Internet search revealed a Smiling Duck Café that already exists. Nuts! Perhaps we should open the Blue Toe Café instead. I'll get back to you.

A bird's ability to survive a New England winter is mind-boggling. Birds are outside in the coldest weather and they never go inside to warm up. They don't get to sit beside a crackling fire, wrapped in a Snuggie and drinking a hot toddy. However, most songbirds can find a sheltered spot for the night. Some crawl into tree cavities, while others hunker down in dense thickets to get away from the biting wind.

Ducks aren't so lucky. They are out there, exposed to the worst weather 24/7, and the best they can do is tuck their bills into their feathers. If that isn't bad enough, they have to spend the entire winter in icy water. Could it get any worse? I'm such a wimp that if the sleeves of my Snuggie get wet when I brush my teeth, I have to put on a new one or I'm freezing for the rest of the night. (I always keep a closet filled with extra Snuggies for such emergencies.)

While ducks may not have access to the same things that keep humans warm, they have something better—down. With all our technology, we still haven't produced anything that insulates as well as duck down, the fluffy feathers found beneath a duck's tough outer feathers. The little pockets of air in the down not only trap body heat, but the trapped air also helps keep the bird buoyant, allowing it to float effortlessly on the water.

Unfortunately, ducks don't have down on their legs and feet. They must spend the entire winter barefoot. I'm sure they'd love to have some leg warmers or a new pair of Uggs, but in order to cut costs, nature has given ducks a less fashionable option. The blood moving to and from their feet circulates in what biologists call a "countercurrent." (FYI, countercurrent should not be confused with "counterculture," which is what you find in places like the Blue Toe Café.)

If we are outside in the cold too long, our bodies slowly restrict blood flow to our extremities. This keeps the body's core temperature from dropping, helping prevent hypothermia. That's a good thing. But with no blood flowing to our feet and hands, we become susceptible to frostbite. That's not such a good thing. To avoid getting frostbite, we go inside; wild ducks have a system of heat exchange, or countercurrent, in which veins and arteries wrap around each other. As the blood flows from a duck's heart, it warms the cold blood returning from the feet. This procedure moderates the incoming blood and keeps the duck's core from becoming chilled and hypothermic. Who knew ducks were so complicated?

The other reason ducks can run around barefoot is mentioned in your question. They have, as you said, "little thin feet." Their feet are thin because they contain few muscles or soft tissue. Long tendons control their feet while most of their muscles are higher up in the legs, kept nice and warm by feathers. It is estimated that only five percent of a duck's body heat is lost through its feet. Don't forget ducks have the ability to withdraw their feet and keep one or both tucked in their feathers, further cutting heat loss.

I'm not saying winter is easy for ducks; it certainly isn't. But they've evolved some effective survival strategies. If you're still worried about your ducks, Julia, invite them in for a cup of coffee, hot chocolate, or even a hot toddy. Just don't offer them a glass of Cold Duck. That would be wrong on so many levels.

The Twelve Days of Christmas Explained, Finally

Dear Bird Folks,

Every year my family argues over the lyrics of the song "The Twelve Days of Christmas." The line of contention is the "four calling birds." Some family members insist it is "four collie birds." We have a house filled with bird books and there are no collie birds in any of them, yet the fight continues. This year we've all agreed to let you decide who is right. Is it calling or collie?

—*Donna,* LAKELAND, FL

Nice, Donna,

I like that your family fights about a Christmas song. My family usually argues over something more emotionally charged, like which grown-up has to eat at the kids' table. What an ugly battle. I pretend I don't want to sit there, but the truth is it's my favorite place to be. I can eat with elbows on the table, use my sleeve as a

napkin, and not have to listen to the adults discuss their doctor appointments.

I've never understood the affection for "The Twelve Days of Christmas." With the exception of the five gold rings, does anybody want that stuff? Try handing your true love three French hens and see what happens. I like birds, but even I wouldn't want three hens, French or otherwise. They are way too messy. I have enough to do cleaning up around the kids' table, especially after I've eaten there.

Can you imagine the complaints from your neighbors if you filled your house with twelve drummers, *all* drumming? How about eleven pipers? Who wants to hear piping? Nine ladies dancing doesn't sound bad, but ten lords a-leaping seems like an accident waiting to happen. Who needs a lawsuit at Christmas?

About calling versus collie birds: I hate to spoil the holiday, but both are wrong. It is "colly" birds. A calling bird would be awful. As anyone who has a pet parrot or peacock can tell you, the constant sound of any bird calling gets old quickly. Collie bird is also wrong. You can look through all the books you want and you won't find a single bird that resembles a collie. Can you imagine a tiny Lassie flying around your head chirping every time Timmy falls in a well?

Colly means grimy or sooty, like a chimney sweep. Colly birds are blackbirds. That's right, blackbirds. Again, the true love is stuck with another lousy gift. However, the blackbirds aren't the same blackbirds that folks here complain about. Even this song isn't suggesting giving someone a pile of grackles or Red-winged Blackbirds for Christmas. These are European blackbirds, which are thrushes, not blackbirds. Confused? Now you know why no one has ever tried to explain it before. Thanks for making me be the one.

A few years ago my wife and I took trip to England. While she was maxing out her credit card at Harrods, I was off looking for birds. (No big surprise there.) One bird caught my attention. It was black like a crow, but much smaller. It didn't behave like a crow either. It was on the lawn of a local park, running in short bursts and stopping every few feet to dig for worms. Its body shape and behavior reminded me of our American Robin. It even had a bright yellow bill, just like a robin does. A quick check of my book told me that this black robin-looking bird is called "Blackbird." It looked and behaved like our robin because it's related to our robin. Both are in the thrush family. In an odd twist, England has a robin but it's not related to our robin, while none of our blackbirds are related to their Blackbird. (I said it was odd, not interesting.)

I hope this puts an end to your annual family feud, Donna. A colly bird is just another name for the European Blackbird, even though it really is a thrush. But no matter what kind of bird it is, it's still a lousy Christmas gift to receive from your true love.

How Could Anyone Be Afraid of a Chickadee?

Dear Bird Folks,
I bought my aunt a bird feeder for her birthday. Upon opening it, her face became pale, she closed the box, and handed it back to me. My uncle explained that she has a fear of birds and would never use the feeder. How could anyone be afraid of a goldfinch or a chickadee?
—*Niki,* CHARLESTON, SC

It's okay, Niki,

Although I'm not happy to hear that someone doesn't like to feed birds, I'm not about to make fun of your aunt for being afraid of anything. People with phobias don't have to explain themselves to me or anyone else. A phobia is an "irrational fear." By definition it doesn't have to make sense. If it made sense, it wouldn't be a phobia. (See, even I can be sympathetic sometimes.)

Lots of people have phobias. In case you are wondering, fear of birds is called "ornithophobia." Fear of heights is "acrophobia." Fear of tight spaces is "claustrophobia." Fear of jumping out of open windows is "Wallstreetophobia." My son has a case of "blankscreenophobia"—fear that the cable might go out. And my wife has "nobagophobia"—fear of leaving a store empty-handed.

No one knows why people become afraid of birds, but that doesn't mean they don't try to come up with reasons. One explanation has to do with the fact that many birds are scavengers. The first ones to attend to dead or dying farm animals are often hungry birds. During the Black Plague, it became impossible to keep up with all the dead bodies, and the birds were more than happy to help themselves to whoever hadn't been buried yet.

Doctors who attended the sick would dress in long black coats and wear beak-shaped masks to filter out the germs and the smell. It was never a good thing when a beak-wearing doctor visited your bedside. Because of these situations, many people saw birds as a sign of bad news. I have relatives in Ireland who won't even allow a picture of a bird into their homes . . . unless, of course, the picture is on a bottle of Wild Turkey.

Crows, blackbirds, starlings, and other birds can form huge, noisy roosting flocks that sometimes invade residential neighborhoods. Spending a week or two with a massive flock of birds squawking overhead could give anyone a permanent case of the bird heebie-jeebies. Edgar Allan Poe, in his creepy poem "The Raven," did little to improve the image of birds. Then there is Alfred Hitchcock, who put the bird movement back decades with his 1963 horror film *The Birds*. And let's not forget the dreaded bird flu, a threat cable news stations remind us of anytime they can't think of anything to say about Britney, Lindsay, or a Kardashian.

If you're like me and can't get enough of watching people break their necks on trampolines, you probably watch *America's Funniest Videos* religiously. In addition to trampolines, there are lots of videos of little kids getting their french fries stolen by gulls or having their noses chomped on by pet parrots, while their parents laugh and continue filming. As funny as that is (and it *is* funny), it also stands to reason that some of these kids might end up visiting their local shrink with a case of ornithophobia.

I don't know your aunt, Niki, but I doubt if she was around during the Black Plague. However, she could have been weirded out by reading "The Raven," seeing *The Birds*, or losing some fries to gulls on a trip to Hilton Head. Whatever the reason, unless it interferes with her enjoyment of life, the cause of the problem and/or resolving it probably isn't that important to her. For example, I have ophidioophobia (fear of snakes) and I'm fine with it. Being afraid of snakes makes perfect sense to me. The only phobia I'd like to see cured is my wife's chronic case of nobagophobia. Curing that would save me thousands.

Even Scary Places Have Birds

Dear Bird Folks,
I wrote to you in 2005 during my first tour of duty in Afghanistan. Now I'm back again. (Lucky me.) During my downtime I try to study the Afghan birds. I found a poster of the area's birds, but it only has the Latin names. One bird, called Upupa epops, *looks like a bird that my wife and I saw in South Africa. Can you tell me what bird* Upupa epops *is?*
—*George,* U.S. ARMY, KABUL, AFGHANISTAN

That's easy, George,

It's easy to decipher a bird's Latin name. Just download the Latin-to-bird translator app onto your iPhone. If you don't have an iPhone, head over to the Apple Store. I'm sure there's one

nearby. It's usually next to a Starbucks, so just look for that. Wait!
You're in Kabul. Never mind. The Apple Store in Kabul probably
isn't open yet.

George, it is good to hear from you again. I was hoping the
next time I heard from you, you'd be at a different address, someplace more like Chicago and less like Kabul. But I'm glad you're
okay and still enjoying birds. I think looking at birds helps lots of
people get through the day. So let's do that right now.

The common name of *Upupa epops* is "Hoopoe." No kidding.
I know Hoopoe sounds like a Native American tribe or a forgotten Marx brother, but that's the bird's name. Why Hoopoe? The
Hoopoe gets its funny-sounding name from its song. It makes
sense. I mean, what else are they going to call a bird that says
"hoop, hoop, hoop" all day long?

If you think the Hoopoe has an odd name, you should see the
bird itself. (I understand you have seen it, George. In this case,
"you" refers to everyone else who hasn't had the good fortune to
visit Kabul.) Hoopoes are about the size of a Blue Jay, and have

buff-pink bodies and flashy black and white wings. Their coloring alone would be enough to make any bird stand out, but the heads of these unusual birds really set them apart. Hoopoes have long, slightly downward curved beaks and thin feathers trailing out the back of their heads. With a long beak in the front and feathers sticking out the back, its head looks like a pickaxe with eyes.

That's strange enough, but it's not the most interesting feature of the Hoopoe's head. When this bird becomes annoyed, its head feathers turn into an enormous, colorful crest. Suddenly the bird looks as if it has a brilliant fan on its head. When I say "fan," I'm not talking about ceiling fans or sports fans but the kind of fans shapely dancers use in burlesque shows. (Most of you probably knew what kind of fan I meant, but I wanted to give George a little excitement. I don't think there's much burlesque in Kabul.)

Usually, with a bird as distinctive as Hoopoes, some mutton-head comes along and tries to capture and cage them all, which ultimately leads to their demise. This is not the case with the Hoopoe. With an estimated population of five million, they are clearly holding their own. Hoopoes can be found throughout much of Africa, Europe, and Asia. In many locations they are fairly easy to find because these birds actually like people, or at least don't totally hate us.

Hoopoes often come to farms, gardens, and parks in search of food. Looking for food is where their pickaxe-shaped heads come into play. Hoopoes use those long, downward-curved beaks to probe the soil for worms and insect larvae. When they find something good hiding below the surface, they jam their beaks into the ground. With their beaks lodged in the dirt, they use their powerful jaw muscles to spread their mandibles and grab the grub. Don't ask me how they can extract food without also getting a beakful of dirt. That's a question for your landscaper.

In some locations Hoopoes are migratory, while in other areas they are permanent residents, but they are basically the same birds throughout their range. That means the birds in Afghanistan and the ones you saw five thousand miles away in South Africa are the same species.

I wish we had Hoopoes in the States. But what I really wish is that you were in the States, George. As soon as you return, I'll take you to an Apple Store and buy you a new iPhone. Wait! I think you misread that. What I wrote was, "I'll buy you a cup of coffee at the Starbucks next door."

Red Squirrels, the Overlooked Annoyance

Dear Bird Folks,

A few years ago I bought a squirrel-proof bird feeder from you, and much to my surprise, it does the job. Try as they might, the gray squirrels have not been able to eat from it. However, that changed last week when a red squirrel arrived in my yard. Now it sits in the feeder, eats away, and screams at anything that tries to interrupt him. Where did this creature come from, and how can I keep it out of my feeder?

—*Scott,* MYSTIC, CT

Don't be so surprised, Scott,

Your line "much to my surprise, it [the feeder] does the job" is a little hurtful. Some of the stuff we sell actually does what it's supposed to. Not everything we offer is a rip-off. But I understand your skepticism. Last week I saw an ad in the paper promoting "invisible fences." Talk about a scam. How would you know if it was actually installed? Maybe I should start selling invisible stuff. Think of the storage room I'd save. Invisible birdseed would help my tired back. Anytime a bird landed in a tree, I could tell people it's eating from an invisible bird feeder. I'd sell millions. I have to get working on this.

The American Red Squirrel is one lucky creature. While the entire human race curses its larger cousin, the gray squirrel, Little Red gets away with murder, sometimes literally (more on that later). The bird-feeding industry has spent millions designing feeders to keep out gray squirrels (with moderate success), but they haven't spent a dime on the red issue. It's a clear case of discrimination.

For anyone who hasn't had the pleasure of dealing with a red squirrel, let me fill you in. Red squirrels are small tree squirrels. They are fluffy and red, looking like a cross between a chipmunk and the thing that lives on Donald Trump's head (only they aren't as cute as the former or as creepy as the latter). They are energetic and feisty, and both descriptions are understatements. Red squirrels have the energy of yapping terrier, combined with the patience of a Tasmanian devil. (It has been estimated that the energy produced by one red squirrel could power a small town, but big oil has kept that a secret.)

Red Squirrels are often referred to as "pine squirrels" because their life revolves around pine trees and pinecones. They harvest green pinecones by chewing them off the branch, then stashing them in a hidden location for later use. It's easy to tell if red squirrels are in your area because you'll find large piles of shredded pinecones, called "middens." I have nothing else to say about middens. I just felt like tossing in a random fact.

In addition to pine seeds, they eat nuts and occasionally bird eggs, young birds, and baby rabbits. (Here's the "getting away with murder" part I mentioned. I know eating rabbits doesn't constitute murder, but tell that to the rabbits.) Before we start thinking these squirrels are barbarians, you should know they also have a sophisticated side. Red squirrels have an appetite for mushrooms. However, they don't eat them fresh. They carry the mushrooms up a tree, place them on a branch and allow them to dry in the sun and become more flavorful before they eat them . . . or before sautéing them with baby rabbit.

So far, we've learned what a midden is and that red squirrels are gourmet cooks. But how do we keep them off our feeders? The answer isn't easy. That's why it has taken me so long to get to it. Most squirrel-proof feeders operate on either one or two principles, both of which are designed with the gray squirrel in mind. A feeder either closes when a squirrel sits on it or has a wire cage around it, which allows the small birds inside to eat but keeps the fat squirrels out. Like chipmunks, red squirrels are often too light to close a feeder when they sit on it. They are also small enough to fit through most wire cages. This fact is not only annoying to anyone who feeds birds, but is equally annoying to me because I have to listen to folks complain about it.

The best way to keep a gray or red squirrel off a feeder is a squirrel baffle. (And I'm talking about a real baffle, not a used salad bowl or trash can cover.) Red squirrels can't get around them. A squirrel baffle designed for a pole or to be hung off a tree branch will do the trick, Scott. Just remember, squirrels are great jumpers. Neither baffle will work unless it is placed at least five feet above the ground and ten feet from the nearest tree, bush, fence, or midden.

If you can't find a baffle in your area, give me a call. I have invisible squirrel baffles coming in next week. I'll give you a good deal on one. Honest.

Stick with Who You Know

Dear Bird Folks,
Do many birds mate for life? I'm sure you've addressed this before
but if you have, I don't recall the answer.

—*Maryanne,* KNOXVILLE, TN

I agree, Maryanne,

I could have sworn I wrote about birds mating for life several times. But after searching through my massive database (the pile of newspaper clippings on my desk), I couldn't find a single column on the topic. I hoped I could answer your question by sending in an old column and going back to bed. But I probably should get up. It's almost suppertime, and I don't want to miss it. I've already slept through breakfast and lunch.

When it comes to pair bonding, birds aren't much different than humans; they have a wide spectrum of relationships. Some birds remain together until death do them part. Other bird couples only stay together for the sake of the children; once the kids go, so do the parents. Some birds don't even wait for the kids to grow up before they take off, leaving the other parent to do the incubating, care giving, and transportation to soccer games.

The Great Horned Owl is a species that probably mates for life. Once paired up, both the male and female birds remain on their joint territory year-round. They don't migrate or go on vacation. If another owl tries to move into their territory, it is quickly driven off . . . or eaten. Really. (Don't ever have an affair with a Great Horned Owl.)

House Wrens have a different approach. The super-hyper male quivers his wings and chatters his song in hopes of attracting a female. Even if he manages to get lucky, the romance may not last. Newly formed wren couples may only remain together long enough for the chicks to fledge. Female wrens have been known to leave their hubbies to finish the job while they head off to start a new family with different males. (This has reality show written all over it.)

Tom turkeys are among the superstuds of the bird world. They have no interest in pair bonding with anything, except themselves. Even a one-night stand is too much of a commitment for them. During the breeding season a tom will mate with as many females as he can attract, or until he passes out. The hens do all the work from that point on.

Chickadee pair formation is interesting. In winter, chickadees live in flocks that consist of a dominant male and dominant female, plus many subordinate birds. Come springtime, the flock breaks up, with most birds pairing off based on their flock ranking. When it's time to breed, the dominant male and female birds fly off together, followed by the next-highest-ranked birds on the chickadee corporate ladder. Rarely will a top-of-the-list female mate with a bottom-of-the-list male. Only human females seem to do that.

Most of us have a soft spot for cardinals. We embrace the idea of Mr. and Mrs. Cardinal spending their life together, and often that is true. However, there is a limit to what these birds will put up with. Birds pair up to produce more birds. They don't need each other to take out the garbage, cook fancy meals, or give backrubs. If a cardinal couple fails to successfully produce a brood, divorce rumors fly; if they don't produce offspring, cardinals rarely remain together.

Mating for life is fairly uncommon in the bird world. Even the birds that breed together in consecutive years don't necessarily spend the winters together. The only time they like to see each other is when it's breeding time. (I think we all know human couples like that.) Also, birds we think are monogamous aren't as pure as they seem; DNA studies have shown that a large percentage of birds stray. While the male guards the front door, his old lady slips out the back to hook up with a friendly neighbor. This might seem sleazy, but it actually benefits the birds. The "friendly neighbor" is often an especially fit male. The more chicks this Romeo can sire, the stronger the species will be.

I'd like to write more, Maryanne, but my wife needs me to take out the garbage. I'd better do it or there might not be any fancy meals for me, and there definitely won't be any backrubs.

Scary Owls

Dear Bird Folks,
We were putting up our Halloween decorations, and as I was hanging up a cardboard cutout of an owl, it made me wonder what owls have to do with Halloween. Ghosts and witches make sense, but why owls?

—*Erica,* MUNCIE, IN

Oh, boo, Erica,

Don't take this the wrong way, but I hate questions that require me to look stuff up. Off the top of my head I can tell you what owls eat, where they like to sleep, and how far they can safely spin their heads around before they need a chiropractor. But I'll

have to do some digging to find out why owls are included in variety packs of Halloween decorations. Those packs always have the same items. In addition to the ghosts and witches you mentioned, let's not forget about those other scary staples: skeletons, bats, and—the most menacing of them all—cats.

But why owls? Owls are soft, warm, and fluffy, and just because they can rip the head off a live animal and eat it in total darkness shouldn't make them scary. Or does it? (If you reread that last line with the sounds of ominous organ music and a sinister laugh playing in your head, it will have the effect I was going for.)

Owls are found all over the world, and just about every civilization has interacted with them. Apparently these nocturnal creatures made the local folks jumpy right from the start because early cave drawings have depicted owls in a menacing manner. The Romans, being educated, saw owls differently. They knew owls were birds of the night and they were cool with that. However, the Romans would freak out if they saw an owl during the day. A daytime sighting was a bad omen, especially if a major battle was imminent. The fall of the Roman Empire probably can be attributed to some insomniac owl that left its roost early.

The French couldn't decide. They liked owls that had ear tufts, but owls without ear tufts made them nervous. Tufted owls were considered symbols of wisdom, but an owl with no ears was a sign of evil. The rare Van Gogh Owl only had one ear tuft and it totally confused everybody.

Some parts of Africa also had owl issues. In part of what is now the Democratic Republic of the Congo, owls were thought to be the cause of illness and therefore, labeled "witchbirds." Being afraid of owls is one thing. But in this part of Africa, the witchbirds were persecuted to such a degree that one species, the Congo Bay-owl, was driven to extinction . . . at least temporarily. In 1951, the last-known Congo Bay-owl was killed, and that was that until 1996, when a female Congo Bay-owl was caught and identified by a researcher. That's great news, but I'll bet the locals aren't thrilled to have the witchbird back. But it could be worse; they could have to deal with the freaky Van Gogh Owl.

In Malaysia, it was believed owls ate newborn babies. This isn't much of stretch. Great Horned Owls have been known to take prey as large as a woodchuck; it is conceivable that a large owl could go after a newborn. However, I don't think that's a good reason to be upset with the owl. If owls are eating your kids, it's time to think about getting a new babysitter.

The origins of Halloween can be traced to Ireland, Scotland, or one of those other damp, foggy countries. At the end of every summer, the locals would have a festival for the dead. During the festival it was thought the separation between the present world and the afterworld became thin and thus the spirits, good and evil, could pass between the two worlds. In order to hide from the evil spirits, people wore masks to conceal their identity. Get it? Masks? Halloween? Since both Ireland and Scotland have strong negative owl superstitions, it's a safe bet that owl images would somehow be involved in a festival for the dead.

Our association with owls and the spooky time of Halloween dates back centuries, Erica. I hope the above info helped explain things. Just don't ask me why people started giving out yummy candy on Halloween. I don't know, but I'm sure glad they do.

Don't Give Kids "Bird Stuff"

Dear Bird Folks,
My ten-year-old granddaughter is interested in birds, and I'd like to encourage her to continue with this hobby. I'm thinking about giving her a box of bird stuff for Christmas. What items do you suggest I include?

—*Paul,* BLOOMINGTON, MN

Good idea, Paul,

I love that you are encouraging your granddaughter's birding hobby. I'd like to say my own kids are interested in birds, but the only birds they can identify are the NBC peacock and Sam, the Fruit Loops toucan. However, I wouldn't refer to your gift as a box of "bird stuff." Bird stuff is what we wash off our cars. I think "birding kit" would be better, but she's your granddaughter so the phrasing is up to you.

The first item in a birding kit should be a bird feeder. Feeders come in four basic styles: cheap and flimsy, artsy-fartsy, squirrel-proof, and plain but made well. Forget the cheap and artsy-fartsy feeders. They won't last long, and the kid could get discouraged before she starts. Squirrel-proof feeders are great but not inexpensive. I have a lot of suggestions for this kit; no sense blowing the budget on one item. A simple, well-made tube feeder with metal perches and seed ports is the way to go. These feeders will last forever. So what if the squirrels can eat out of it? Let your granddaughter learn about squirrels the hard way, like the rest of us. It will build character.

Of course, you'll need food for the feeder, and that should be sunflower seed. If you dare buy your granddaughter a bag of that mixed crap from the grocery store, I'll report you to DSS. The next item is a good field guide. There are many "beginner" books out there, but I'm not a fan of watered-down bird books, even for kids. Everyone, at any age, should have a complete birding field guide. I hear too many adults misnaming birds because the bird they saw wasn't in *Little Billy's Guide to Pretty Birds*. Get an all-inclusive book. Or buy her a beginner's book and a comprehensive book for her parents. That way, there'll be at least one good book in the kid's house.

If you intend to buy your granddaughter binoculars, Paul, here are some guidelines. Many birders don't recommend small, compact binoculars, but in this case small makes sense. No ten-year-old girl wants to drag around heavy binoculars. Plus, small binoculars fit better in small hands. But don't even think about buying her binoculars made by Fisher-Price or Mattel. Binoculars aren't supposed to have pictures of SpongeBob or Hello Kitty (definitely not that!) on them.

I'm not saying you have to get top-of-the-line optics, but at least buy a brand name. You should also look through them first to make sure they work. That means you shouldn't consider binoculars that come in those frustrating plastic clamshell packs. Not only won't you be able to try them first, but your granddaughter will be in college by the time she figures out how to get the package open.

One thing younger people have that many adults don't have is good hearing. Because of that I would encourage you to consider a CD of bird songs. Identifying birds is a million times easier if you can recognize songs and calls. And unlike my complete bird-book rant earlier, a bird-song CD doesn't need to include every bird. A good collection of backyard bird songs is fine for a young birder. Let her master familiar songs first. See, I can be flexible.

The last thing you should purchase is the most important item of all. Buy your granddaughter a new fire-red Corvette convertible, the perfect vehicle for birding. You can see and hear the birds so much better in a car without a roof. Because your granddaughter is only ten, I'll keep this car safe for her until she's old enough to drive. I would totally do that for you, Paul. That's the kind of guy I am.

Turkeys Rule, Eagles Drool

Dear Bird Folks,
This may be a colonial version of an urban legend, but I read that
Benjamin Franklin lobbied for the Wild Turkey to be our national
bird instead of the Bald Eagle. Is that true?

—*Craig,* KINGSTON, NY

No, Craig,

Franklin never lobbied for the turkey. How's that for an instant answer? I'm in a hurry this week.

While it's true that Ben wasn't happy with the choice of the
Bald Eagle for our national bird, it's unlikely he "lobbied" on be-
half of the turkey. Most turkey lovers spin the story differently but
my sources, who shall remain anonymous, paint another picture
of how this all went down.

After Congress made its decision, Franklin merely suggested
that the turkey would have been a better choice. In his eyes, the
eagle was nothing more than a scrounge and a mooch, and in
some ways he was right. Bald Eagles do hunt, but they often scav-
enge and are happy to steal food from any creature they can.

Franklin may not have lobbied for the Wild Turkey over the
eagle, but I wish he had. To begin with, the Bald Eagle isn't even
bald. Its head is covered in white feathers. Claiming to be bald
just to impress Congress is clearly fraudulent. The Wild Turkey, on
the other hand, truly is bald and proud of it. Like Kojak and Mr.
Clean, the turkey's baldness makes it more self-confident. It struts
around with its chest puffed out, ready to take on all comers. It's
the perfect image for a cocky new country.

Speaking of feathers, the Bald Eagle has nothing but a basic
color scheme: brown feathers and white feathers, and that's it.
Pitiful. The turkey has a large variety of colored feathers. Its huge

tail can be fanned out to display an assortment of rust, tan, and warm brown shading, while its body is some kind of indescribable metallic color. But its head really sets it apart from most other birds. Depending on the mood or attitude, the coloring of the bird's face can change from white to red to blue. Yes, red, white, and blue. How much more patriotic can a bird get? A turkey's face also has something important that no eagle has: a hunk of skin—a snood—hanging from its forehead. After the American Revolution, this country was desperate to impress other nations, especially England. Nothing would have impressed the Brits more than knowing our national bird had its own snood.

In a race, a turkey would blow an eagle away. While the turkey can run in excess of 20 mph, the best an eagle can do on land is stumble about. Eagles can't run, and they walk awkwardly, as if they are wearing another bird's shoes . . . on the wrong feet. Turkeys are capable of flight speeds approaching 55 mph. Though an eagle may fly over 100 mph, it can only hit those speeds in a dive with gravity doing most of the work. It doesn't deserve points for that.

Many eagle lovers may say the eagle's hunting skills are a sign of bravery and toughness. After all, eagles can catch and eat animals as large as a raccoon, a beaver, or a young deer. So what? Wild Turkeys eat mostly vegetable matter. Take it from me: nothing is tougher or braver than facing three vegetarian meals day after day.

When it comes to reproducing, turkeys have it all over eagles. A mother turkey can hatch and raise a dozen or more baby turkeys by herself. In a good year, a Bald Eagle pair will most likely raise only two eaglets. If a third chick should hatch, the big, muscular eagle parents become so overwhelmed they often let the extra chick starve. Nice, eh?

Let's not forget about the turkey trot. Was a dance ever named after a Bald Eagle? I've never heard of the eagle trot. And when we want to be honest and candid, we talk turkey. We don't talk eagle.

Ben Franklin didn't lobby for the Wild Turkey to be our national bird, Craig, but he should have. It's a better choice. However, even I have to admit that when he landed on the moon, if instead of saying, "Houston . . . the Eagle has landed," Neil Armstrong had said, "Houston . . . the Turkey has landed," it would have lost some historical impact. But it would have been funnier.

Start the Year with a Bird List . . . Instead of a Hangover

Dear Bird Folks,
My New Year's resolution is to start a bird list. Any advice?
—*Ned,* MASHPEE, MA

It's easy, Ned,
Get a pad of paper. When you see a bird, write it down. When you see a different bird, repeat step 2. I told you it was easy.

What else do you want to talk about? We'd better think of something, or this will be a short column. I know. What did you get for Christmas? Anything good? I'll bet you can't top what I got. My wife gave me a laundry bag. A laundry bag? Isn't that what the floor is for? My wife is probably still mad about the frying pan I gave her last year. How was I supposed to know she already had one? She was happier this Christmas when I gave her a new paint scraper. Our holidays are practical.

Even though your question didn't require a long answer, Ned, I like your New Year's resolution. It's a lot less stressful than the ones we typically make for ourselves. Besides, no one ever does any of those things they say they are going to do: lose weight, exercise more, or put their dirty clothes into a laundry bag. With that in mind, here are a few goals that backyard bird watchers might want to accomplish in the New Year.

The first one is simple. Identify one new bird eating from your feeder. That's all. I suggest this because many people have no idea what species of birds are eating their expensive birdseed. Every day I ask folks if they are getting a lot of birds. They usually say, "Tons." When I ask them to name a few of the birds their faces go blank, like escapees from Madame Tussauds. After some deep thought, they say, "I get the regular birds." (Judging from the hood of my car, being "regular" is not a problem for birds.) If they paid a little attention, I bet most people would be surprised at the number of different birds coming to their feeders.

Go for a bird walk in a new location. Get out your map and find a new place to walk and explore. The key words here are "walk" and "explore." Where I live, too many people (usually men) drive to the beach or some beautiful spot and sit in the car with the engine running and read the paper. That's not bird watching. It's just lame.

Plan a day of birding while you're on vacation instead of spending every day frying on a tropical beach or playing another stupid round of golf. Cardinals and chickadees are fine, but perhaps it's time to see some of the world's ten thousand other species of birds. No matter where you travel to, there will always be good birding spots nearby. Check 'em out. Remember to pack your binoculars and bird books. They may add a little weight to your suitcase, but they are way lighter and more useful than golf clubs.

Your idea about starting a bird list is a good one, Ned. Many hardcore birders use complicated computer programs or intricate notebook lists, but that seems too corporate. Birding should be fun and not filled with mounds of paperwork. Keeping a simple list of new birds may be the motivation we need to go outside and do more birding.

In fact, going outside more often is just what I recommend to my wife. There's nothing like a day of sunshine, fresh air, and paint scraping.

Casey O'Connor

For more than thirty years, **Mike O'Connor** has owned and operated the Bird Watcher's General Store on Cape Cod, and every day he answers hundreds of questions about birds (and zillions of complaints about squirrels). His column, "Ask the Bird Folks," appears in the *Cape Codder*, as well as in several of the Cape's other weekly newspapers. Mike was a contributor to *Good Birders Don't Wear White*, a book featuring birding tips from fifty of the country's top birders, and he has a regular Q&A segment on Ray Brown's syndicated radio show *Talkin' Birds*. His segment is coincidentally entitled "Let's Ask Mike." O'Connor's first book, *Why Don't Woodpeckers Get Headaches?*, has been well received by birders at every level and was the number-one-selling book at his store for nearly an entire week. (That's something Mike is very proud of.) When he isn't answering questions or hoisting bags of birdseed for his customers, Mike is looking for birds, which is why he always keeps his binoculars handy.

185